Foreword

We are delighted to welcome a reprint of "101 Square Meals" which has proven a wonderful and valuable resource for individuals and families in the home and also for those delivering home management educational programmes in the community. The presentation and layout is innovative and appeals to new as well as seasoned cooks.

This Book was designed to accommodate two considerations i.e. budget and nutrition. Irish healthy eating guidelines encourage people to eat a wide variety of foods based around the food pyramid. Research shows that on average people are eating too many high fat foods and not taking enough fruit and vegetables. The cook book provides clear and simple to follow recipes which encourage people to reduce fat in their everyday meals and support the philosophy of affordable good nutrition. In this context it is great to see Limerick MABS continuing in its pioneering role of producing materials dealing with money management.

Finally we would like to congratulate Limerick MABS, the Mid-Western Health Board and the PAUL Partnership on developing this valuable resource and are delighted that our respective Community & Voluntary and Health Promotion Units, in both Departments, are associated with "101 Square Meals".

Happy and healthy cooking for you and your families.

Dermot Ahern T.D.
Minister for Social
Community and Family Affairs

Michael Martin T.D.
Minister for Health
and Children

Introduction

This publication recognises a critical aspect of domestic budget management, i.e., purchasing and preparing nutritious food. It is a response to a need identified by the Limerick Money Advice and Budgeting Service and the Health Promotion Unit of the Mid-Western Health Board as part of their remit to produce resource materials relating to money management and healthy eating.

The aim of this cookery book is to provide easy-to-prepare, low-budget, yet highly nutritious meals. It also contains useful tips on shopping, home freezing and food hygiene. Hopefully this will result in healthier, more balanced diets for families and individuals and a reduction in their food bills.

In this edition, you will find a newly updated section on weaning that reflects the very latest recommendations for your baby. There is also a new section, which provides a practical guide and creative ideas on healthy eating for young people. These welcome additions ensure that the book continues to offer the best and most up to date advice, and that it will be a valuable support in the national campaign against obesity.

The '101' recipes offer variety for every age and circumstance.

Compiled by Norah Bourke, with contributions by
Sheila King and Marie Flanagan.

contents

Breakfasts

Sauces and Soups

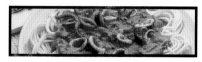

Mince Dishes

Beef Loaf	18
Burgers - Quick	19
Chilli Con Carne	20
Hot Pot - Creamy	21
Lasagne	22
Minced Beef and Vegetable Pie	23
Spaghetti Bolognese	24
Spicy Meatballs	25

Beef/Lamb/Pork

Beef Casserole	27
Beef/Lamb Curry	28
Beef Goulash	29
Beef Stew	30
Lamb Cutlet Casserole	31
Liver Hot-Pot	32
Pork Casserole	33
Pork Stir-Fry	34
Stuffed Pork Chops in Foil	35

Fish

Baked Stuffed Fish	37
Chip Shop Fish Supper	38
Crispy Baked Cod in Tomato Sauce	39
Family Fish Pie	40
Fish Cakes	41
Fritter Batter	42
Golden Cod	43
Salmon Surprise	44
Tuna Quick Bake	45

Chicken

Vegetarian

Cakes

Snacks

Weaning

Young people

Notes

Sponsors

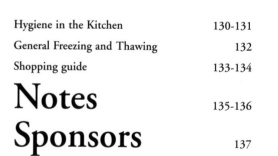

Recipe Symbols

FRY	OVEN	CASSEROLE	GRILL	BOIL/STEW	DEEP FRY	FRIDGE

HEALTHY

HEALTHIER OPTION

PREPARATION TIME	COOKING TIME
10 minutes	**10** minutes

UTENSILS NEEDED
TYPE OF UTENSILS NEEDED TO COOK THE RECIPE

HANDY HINTS
Usually giving an alternative ingredient or serving suggestion.

LOW COST	MEDIUM COST	HIGH COST

NUMBER OF SERVINGS	
	1 serving
	2 servings
	3 servings
	4 servings
	family

Measurements / Weights

Metric	Imperial	Metric	Imperial
5g	¹/₄ oz./1 teaspoon	250g	9oz
15g	¹/₂ oz./1 dessertspoon	280g	10oz
25g	1oz	300g	11oz
50g	2oz	340g	12oz
85g	3oz	375g	13oz
110g	4oz	400g	14oz
140g	5oz	425g	15oz
180g	6oz	450 g	16oz/1lb
200g	7oz		
225g	8oz		

Metric	Imperial	Metric	Imperial
¹/₄ pt	150ml	³/₄ pt	425ml
¹/₃ pt	200ml	1 pt	575ml
¹/₂ pt	275ml	1³/₄ pts	1 litre

HANDY HINTS

Yoghurt pot measures
Use any standard shape yoghurt pot marked 125g or 5.3oz
One pot is approximately:

4oz	white flour	3oz	wholemeal flour
6oz	castor or granulated sugar	4oz	soft brown sugar

5 fluid oz - liquid (e.g., water, milk)

Oven Temperature Conversion Table

DESCRIPTION	DEG. C	DEG. F	GAS MARK
Cool	110	225	Quarter
Extremely low	120	250	Half
Very low	140	275	1
Low	150	300	2
Very moderate	160	325	3
Moderate	180	350	4
Moderately hot	190	375	5
Fairly hot	200	400	6
Hot	220	425	7
Very hot	230	450	8
Very very hot	240	475	9

Breakfasts

Breakfasts

1	JUICE	Orange/Grapefruit	
2	FRUIT	Oranges/Mandarins, Grapefruit, Bananas	
3	BREAD	Wholemeal, Wholegrain, White Bread	
4	CEREALS	HIGH FIBRE IE.	Porridge
			Wheat Biscuits
			Fruit & Fibre
			Muesli
			Shredded Wheat
			Common-Sense Oatflakes
			Bran Buds
			Sultana Bran
		LOW IN FIBRE IE.	Cornflakes
			Rice Krispies
			Special K
		WEEKEND TREATS, LOW IN FIBRE IE.	Coco Pops
			Sugar Puffs
			Crunchy Nut Cornflakes
			Honey Nut Loops
			Frosties

Suggestions for Cooked Breakfasts

French Toast

INGREDIENTS

4 slices bread 1 egg a little vegetable oil	3 dessertspoons milk salt and pepper	

1. Beat egg, milk, pepper and salt together in a shallow bowl.

2. Dip the slices of bread in the egg mixture.

3. Fry in hot oil until they are golden brown.

4. Drain on kitchen paper.

FRY

COST

NUMBER OF SERVINGS

PREPARATION TIME	COOKING TIME
5 minutes	**5** minutes

UTENSILS NEEDED

FRYING PAN

HANDY HINTS

Serve with grilled sausage and tomato or grilled rasher and tomato.

Omit salt & pepper and serve with a little jam or castor sugar.

FRY

COST	HEALTHY
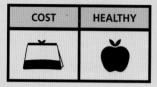	

NUMBER OF SERVINGS

PREPARATION TIME	COOKING TIME
10 minutes	**10** minutes

UTENSILS NEEDED

FRYING PAN

HANDY HINTS

If more than one omelette is required increase the eggs and onion. Fry the mixture and complete cooking under the grill.

Serve with toast.

Omelette

INGREDIENTS		
2 eggs 1 dessertspoon oil salt and pepper	1 small onion, finely chopped 2 dessertspoons water/milk	

1. Heat the oil in a frying pan and fry the onion gently until it is cooked.

2. Beat the eggs, add the water/milk, salt and pepper and pour into the pan over the onion.

3. Spread the mixture around the frying pan and cook until the eggs are set and come away from the edge of the frying pan.

4. Turn the omelette carefully to cook on the other side.

Poached Eggs

INGREDIENTS		
3 eggs	salt and pepper	
1 dessertspoon of vinegar	½ pt/250ml water	

1. Put the water into a saucepan or frying pan, add salt, pepper and vinegar. Bring to the boil.

2. Break the eggs into the boiling salted water. Simmer gently until the eggs are set. About 2 - 3 minutes.

3. Serve with toast and beans.

BOIL/STEW

COST	HEALTHY

NUMBER OF SERVINGS

PREPARATION TIME	COOKING TIME
2 minutes	**3** minutes

UTENSILS NEEDED

SAUCEPAN
FRYING PAN

HANDY HINTS

The vinegar prevents the egg yoke from breaking.

Use metal bun cutters to keep the eggs in shape.

BOIL/STEW

COST	HEALTHY

NUMBER OF SERVINGS

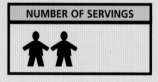

PREPARATION TIME	COOKING TIME
5 minutes	**2-3** minutes

UTENSILS NEEDED

SHALLOW BOWL
WOODEN SPOON
SAUCEPAN

HANDY HINTS

Add grated cheese,
parsley, ham etc.

Scrambled Eggs

INGREDIENTS		
3 eggs 1 dessertspoon oil salt and pepper	4 dessertspoons milk	

1. Break the eggs into a shallow bowl and beat well with a fork.

2. Heat the oil in a saucepan then add the milk, pepper and salt.

3. Add the beaten eggs and stir over a moderate heat until mixture is thick and creamy.

4. Do not cook for too long or it will curdle.

5. Serve on hot toast.

Sauces & Soups

BOIL/STEW

COST

NUMBER OF SERVINGS

PREPARATION TIME	COOKING TIME
2 minutes	**5** minutes

UTENSILS NEEDED

WOODEN SPOON
SAUCEPAN

HANDY HINTS

If the sauce becomes lumpy, place it in a sieve over a pot.
Work the sauce through the sieve into the pot below.
Always use a wooden spoon when preparing sauces.

White Pouring Sauce

INGREDIENTS		
1oz/25g margarine 1oz/25g flour ³/₄ pt/425ml milk	salt and pepper	

(1) Melt the margarine in a saucepan.

(2) Add the flour and cook over a low heat for 1 minute, stirring all the time.

(3) Remove from the heat and cool slightly.

(4) Add the milk, salt and pepper beating all the time.

(5) Return to the heat and bring to the boil. Keep stirring.

(6) Reduce heat and cook slowly for 5 minutes.

Sauces - Various

1 White Coating Sauce
as for pouring sauce but using ¹/₂ pt/275ml milk.

2 Onion Sauce
as for white sauce but fry one finely chopped onion in margarine before adding the flour.

3 Cheese Sauce
as for white pouring sauce but add 2oz/50g grated cheese 2 minutes before the end of the cooking time.

4 Parsley Sauce
as for white pouring sauce but add 1-2 teaspoons of finely chopped parsley 2 minutes before the end of the cooking time.

BOIL/STEW

COST	HEALTHY
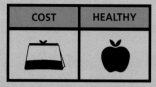	

NUMBER OF SERVINGS

PREPARATION TIME	COOKING TIME
8 minutes	**20** minutes

UTENSILS NEEDED

WOODEN SPOON
SAUCEPAN

HANDY HINTS

*To make chicken stock, simply add a couple of chicken wings or a carcass of a chicken and an onion to 1³/₄ pts/1 litre of water and boil for 1 hour.

Chicken Soup

INGREDIENTS		
1 teaspoon vegetable oil 2oz/50g flour ¹/₂ pt/275ml milk	1 pt/575ml of chicken stock* or 2 stock cubes dissolved in 1pt/575ml of boiling water salt and pepper	1 finely chopped onion

1. Heat the oil in a saucepan.

2. Add the finely chopped onion and fry for 1 minute.

3. Add in the flour and cook for 2 minutes, stirring all the time.

4. Gradually stir in the stock with salt and pepper.

5. Bring to the boil and simmer for 15 minutes, keep stirring until thickened.

Cream of Mushroom Soup

INGREDIENTS

1 teaspoon vegetable oil 10 mushrooms chopped 50g/2oz flour	1 pt/575ml stock or 2 stock cubes dissolved in 1 pt/575ml of boiling water ³/₄ pt/425ml milk	salt and pepper 1 finely chopped onion

1. Heat the oil in a saucepan. Add the mushrooms and onion and fry, stirring continually for 5 minutes.

2. Add the flour and stir well. Cook for another 2 minutes.

3. Gradually stir in the stock and milk and bring to the boil. Keep stirring.

4. Simmer for 20 minutes, until thickened.

5. Add salt and pepper to taste.

COST	HEALTHY

NUMBER OF SERVINGS

PREPARATION TIME	COOKING TIME
8 minutes	**20** minutes

UTENSILS NEEDED

WOODEN SPOON
SAUCEPAN

HANDY HINTS

Corn may be added to this soup.

Farmhouse Vegetable Soup

COST	HEALTHY

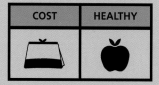

NUMBER OF SERVINGS

PREPARATION TIME	COOKING TIME
15 minutes	**45** minutes

UTENSILS NEEDED

WOODEN SPOON
SAUCEPAN

HANDY HINTS

Not all vegetables here need to be used. Select according to availability, choice and cost.

Avoid using green vegetables e.g., cabbage or brussel sprouts.

INGREDIENTS		
3 carrots 1 turnip 1 parsnip 1-2 leeks 1 onion	8 mushrooms 3 tomatoes/tin of tomatoes 1 teaspoon vegetable oil 2oz/50g flour	$1/4$ pt/150ml milk salt and pepper 2 chicken stock cubes dissolved in $1^{3}/_4$ pts/ 1 litre of water

1. Wash, peel and dice carrots, turnips and parsnips. Wash and chop leeks, chop onion and slice mushrooms. Skin and chop tomatoes.

2. Heat the oil in a large saucepan, and gently fry onion and mushrooms.

3. Add carrots, turnips, parsnips and leeks and fry gently.

4. Stir in the flour to absorb fat, gradually stir in the milk.

5. Add stock and bring to boil, stirring continuously.

6. Add tomatoes, salt and pepper.

7. Cover saucepan and simmer gently for about 45 minutes.

Mince

OVEN

COST	HEALTHY
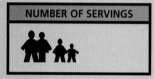	

NUMBER OF SERVINGS

PREPARATION TIME	COOKING TIME
15 minutes	**1½** hours

UTENSILS NEEDED

LARGE LOAF TIN
MIXING BOWL

HANDY HINTS

Serve hot with vegetables.
Serve cold with salad.

Beef Loaf

INGREDIENTS		
1lb/450g minced beef	2 dessertspoons tomato sauce	
1 large onion, very finely chopped	2 beef cubes crumbled and dissolved in ¼ pt/150ml hot water	
4oz/110g fresh white breadcrumbs (4 slices)		
salt and pepper	1 egg, beaten	

1. Pre-heat the oven to 180°C / 350°F / Gas Mark 4.

2. Place all the ingredients in a large mixing bowl and mix thoroughly together.

3. Brush a large loaf tin with oil and fill with the mixture.

4. Smooth the top with a palette knife and place in the fridge for 1 hour.

5. Cook in the pre-heated oven for 1¼-1½ hours.

Burgers - Quick

INGREDIENTS		
1lb/450g minced beef/lamb 4oz/110g breadcrumbs (4 slices)	pinch mixed herbs 1 small onion - finely chopped a little beaten egg	salt and pepper a little flour

1. Mix all the ingredients together in a bowl.

2. Bind with a little beaten egg.

3. Shape mixture into round shapes with a little flour.

4. Fry or grill gently on both sides over a low heat until well cooked.

5. Serve in bread buns or with mashed potato.

COST **HEALTHY**

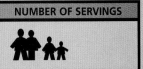

NUMBER OF SERVINGS

PREPARATION TIME | **COOKING TIME**
10 minutes | **20** minutes

UTENSILS NEEDED

MIXING BOWL
FRYING PAN

HANDY HINTS

Add a few drops of Tabasco Sauce to the minced beef mixture for extra flavour.

To ensure that burgers are cooked in the centre, cover the pan with a lid and lower the heat.

Delicious served in pitta breads.

19

COST	HEALTHY

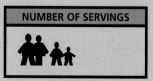

NUMBER OF SERVINGS

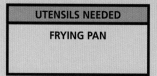

PREPARATION TIME	COOKING TIME
30 minutes	**20** minutes

UTENSILS NEEDED

FRYING PAN

HANDY HINTS

Use a saucepan if frying pan is too small.

Serve with boiled rice or potatoes.

Chilli Con Carne

INGREDIENTS		
1lb/450g of minced beef/lamb	1 beef cube	1 clove of garlic (crushed)
1 onion, finely chopped	1 teaspoon chilli powder	½ tin of kidney beans or tin of baked beans
½ tin tomatoes	2 dessertspoons tomato sauce	1 dessertspoon of flour

1. Chop onion and garlic.
   Dissolve beef cube in a ¼ pt/150ml of boiling water.

2. Put minced beef/lamb in dry frying pan. There is sufficient fat in mince for frying. Cook for 20-25 minutes over a low heat until well browned, stirring all the time.

3. Add onions and garlic to the pan and cook for 2 to 3 minutes. Sprinkle on the flour and chilli powder and cook for 1-2 minutes, stirring all the time.

4. Add beef stock, tomato sauce and tinned tomatoes. Bring to the boil.

5. Add kidney beans/baked beans to mince. Simmer for 20 minutes.

Hot Pot - Creamy

FRY **OVEN**

INGREDIENTS		
1lb/450g minced beef 1 medium onion, finely chopped salt and pepper	1 can of cream of celery soup 1 tablespoon worcestershire sauce	½ pt/275ml milk 4 potatoes peeled and thinly sliced

1. Pre-heat the oven to 200°C / 400°F / Gas Mark 6.

2. Put minced beef and finely chopped onion into a large frying pan and fry until the meat is browned and onion is cooked (about 5 minutes). Keep stirring.

3. Stir in the soup mixture, milk and worcestershire sauce. Simmer gently for 10 minutes. Add salt and pepper.

4. Spoon mixture into casserole dish and top with sliced potatoes.

5. Bake for 30 minutes until the potatoes are tender.

COST **HEALTHY**

NUMBER OF SERVINGS

PREPARATION TIME	COOKING TIME
20 minutes	**30** minutes

UTENSILS NEEDED

FRYING PAN
CASSEROLE DISH

HANDY HINTS

Leek and potato soup can also be used.

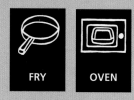

FRY **OVEN**

NUMBER OF SERVINGS

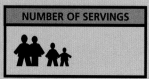

PREPARATION TIME	COOKING TIME
30 minutes	**40** minutes

UTENSILS NEEDED

SAUCEPAN
CASSEROLE DISH

HANDY HINTS

Double the ingredients and make in a large roasting dish.

When cooked divide into individual portions and freeze.

Use a medium sized box of easi-cook lasagne sheets.

Lasagne

INGREDIENTS		
1lb/450g mince beef/lamb 1 onion 1 green or red pepper 8 mushrooms	1 tin chopped tomatoes 2 dessertspoons of tomato sauce salt and pepper	1 clove garlic cheese sauce (see page 13) 10 sheets of easi-cook lasagne sheets

1. Pre-heat the oven to 180°C / 350°F / Gas Mark 4.

2. TO MAKE MEAT SAUCE:
Chop onions, peppers, mushrooms and garlic. Put mince into a large pan and fry until completely brown, stirring all the time with a wooden spoon. Add onions and garlic to mince and cook for 3-4 minutes. Add chopped peppers, chopped mushrooms, tin of tomatoes and tomato sauce to the mince mixture. Bring to the boil and leave to simmer on a low heat for 15-20 minutes.

3. TO MAKE THE CHEESE SAUCE: see page 13.

4. FINAL PREPARATION:
Put layer of meat sauce in the bottom of casserole dish, cover with easi-cook lasagne sheets. Make 1 or 2 more layers as above finishing with a layer of lasagne sheets. Cover with cheese sauce. Sprinkle with remainder of cheese and bake for 30 to 40 minutes.

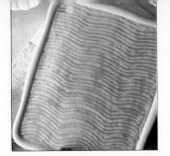

Minced Beef and Vegetable Pie

FRY   BOIL/STEW   OVEN

COST	HEALTHY

INGREDIENTS		
1lb/450g minced beef 1 onion 2 carrots	1 packet of beef and vegetable soup 5 potatoes cooked low fat milk	salt and pepper ³/₄ pt/425ml of cold water

NUMBER OF SERVINGS

PREPARATION TIME	COOKING TIME
20 minutes	**45** minutes

1. Pre-heat the oven to 180°C / 375°F / Gas Mark 4.

2. Place the minced beef in a frying pan. Add salt and pepper.

3. Peel the onion and the carrots and chop them finely. Add to the minced beef.

4. Fry until the meat is browned (approx. 15 mins).

5. Mix the packet of soup powder with ³/₄ pt/425ml of cold water and add to the minced meat.

6. Bring to the boil, stirring all the time.

7. Put into a greased casserole dish.

8. Mash the potatoes and add a little milk and seasoning.

9. Spoon on top of meat mixture and smooth gently with a knife or fork to form a pattern on top.

10. Bake in the pre-heated oven for 45 minutes.

UTENSILS NEEDED

FRYING PAN
CASSEROLE DISH

HANDY HINTS

Use a packet of oxtail soup instead of beef and vegetable soup for tasty shepherd's pie.

COST | HEALTHY

NUMBER OF SERVINGS

PREPARATION TIME	COOKING TIME
15 minutes	**45** minutes

UTENSILS NEEDED

FRYING PAN
SAUCEPAN

HANDY HINTS

Any leftover bolognese sauce can be used to fill pancakes or as a topping for baked potatoes.

Spaghetti Bolognese

INGREDIENTS		
1lb/450g mince beef/lamb	1 dessertspoon tomato sauce	6 mushrooms chopped (optional)
1 onion finely chopped	salt and pepper	8oz spaghetti
beef cube	1 dessertspoon flour	
$^1/_2$ pt/275ml of water	1 tin of tomatoes	

1. Cook the mince beef/lamb, onions and mushrooms on a low heat for 15 minutes. (Sufficient fat in mince for frying).

2. Add flour and stir well.

3. Add the water and before it comes to the boil add the crushed beef cube, tin of tomatoes, tomato sauce, salt and pepper. Cook gently for 45 minutes.

4. Cook the spaghetti for 10-15 minutes in boiling salted water. Strain.

5. Serve with the bolognese sauce on top.

Spicy Meatballs

FRY

INGREDIENTS

1lb/450g minced lamb/beef	2-3 cloves of garlic finely chopped	2 dessertspoons curry powder
1 large onion, finely chopped	1 teaspoon ginger (optional)	1 dessertspoon cornflour/flour

1. Place the minced meat in a large bowl.

2. Fry the onion and garlic until golden brown.

3. Mix the curry powder, ginger and cornflour/flour with a little water and add to the pan. Cook for a few minutes.

4. Add this mixture to the mince meat and mix well.

5. Shape into meatballs with damp hands.

6. Fry gently for 15-20 minutes, turning occasionally.

COST	HEALTHY

NUMBER OF SERVINGS

PREPARATION TIME	COOKING TIME
15 minutes	**20** minutes

UTENSILS NEEDED

FRYING PAN
LARGE BOWL

HANDY HINTS

Omit the curry powder and ginger from the ingredients and make up curry sauce separately and cook the meatballs in it.

Serve with pasta.

Beef / Lamb / Pork

Beef Casserole

FRY   CASSEROLE   OVEN

COST	HEALTHY

NUMBER OF SERVINGS

PREPARATION TIME	COOKING TIME
20 minutes	**1½** hours

UTENSILS NEEDED

FRYING PAN
CASSEROLE DISH

HANDY HINTS

Add 4oz/110g of beef kidney washed and dried for beef and kidney casserole.

INGREDIENTS

1½ lb / 675g round beef steak/rib steak 1 dessertspoon cooking oil 1 large onion, peeled and chopped	1oz / 25g / cornflour 7 mushrooms, sliced 3 carrots, sliced salt and pepper	1 pt/575ml beef stock (2 stock cubes dissolved in 1pt/575ml of warm water) 1 tablespoon tomato puree

1. Pre-heat the oven to 170°C / 325°F / Gas Mark 3.

2. Trim the beef and cut it into thin strips about 2 inches in length.

3. Heat the oil and fry the chopped onion, mushrooms and carrots for 2-3 minutes. Place in casserole dish.

4. Fry the beef strips until brown.

5. Place in the casserole dish.

6. Mix the cornflour with the juice in the pan and cook for 2-3 minutes. Remove from heat and stir in the stock.

7. Bring to the boil, add the tomato puree, salt and pepper.

8. Add to the casserole dish and cook for 1½ hours.

COST	HEALTHY

NUMBER OF SERVINGS

PREPARATION TIME	COOKING TIME
20 minutes	**1½** hours

UTENSILS NEEDED
FRYING PAN CASSEROLE DISH

HANDY HINTS
This can be cooked on top of the cooker in a saucepan over a low heat for 1-1½ hours until the meat is tender. Serve with boiled rice or boiled potatoes.

Beef/Lamb Curry

INGREDIENTS		
1lb/450g stewing beef/lamb 1 large onion chopped 1 clove of garlic chopped	2 dessertspoons curry powder 1oz/25g flour 1 apple, peeled and grated	1¾ pts/1 litre stock (2 beef cubes dissolved in 1¾ pts/1 litre warm water)

1. Pre-heat the oven to 180°C / 350°F / Gas Mark 4.

2. Cut meat into one-inch pieces. Fry the meat, onion and garlic over a low heat until the meat is brown on all sides.

3. Then place in a casserole dish.

4. Add flour and curry powder to the juices remaining in the pan.

5. Cook for 2-3 minutes.

6. Add the stock and grated apple. Stir continuously to avoid lumps.

7. Bring to the boil and add to the meat mixture in casserole.

8. Cook in the pre-heated oven for 1½ hours until meat is tender.

Beef Goulash

FRY

BOIL/STEW

COST	HEALTHY

INGREDIENTS

1½ lb/675g stewing beef	salt and pepper	1 dessertspoon tomato puree
1 dessertspoon cooking oil	2 tomatoes, skinned and chopped	1 pt/575ml water
3 onions, peeled and sliced	1 clove garlic crushed	6-8 potatoes, peeled and sliced
	½ dessertspoon paprika	

NUMBER OF SERVINGS

PREPARATION TIME	COOKING TIME
15 minutes	**1½** hours

UTENSILS NEEDED

FRYING PAN
SAUCEPAN

HANDY HINTS

Stir in 2 dessertspoons of natural yoghurt before serving.

1 Remove the fat from the meat and cut into one-inch cubes.

2 Heat the oil in a large frying pan. Add the cubes of beef a few at a time and fry them until they are brown on all sides.

3 Transfer the browned meat to a saucepan.

4 Fry the onions in the pan until they are golden brown.

5 Stir in the tomatoes, garlic, paprika, tomato puree, salt and pepper.

6 Add this to the browned meat. Then add the water. Bring to boil, stirring all the time.

7 Cover with a lid and cook slowly for 1 hour.

8 Add the sliced potatoes and simmer for another 30 minutes approximately.

COST	HEALTHY

NUMBER OF SERVINGS

PREPARATION TIME	COOKING TIME
15 minutes	**1½** hours

UTENSILS NEEDED

FRYING PAN
SAUCEPAN

HANDY HINTS

Add washed and peeled potatoes to the stew, 30 minutes before the end of cooking time.

This may also be cooked in a casserole in the oven.

Beef Stew

INGREDIENTS		
1½ lb/675g stewing beef 1 dessertspoon vegetable oil	2 beef stock cube dissolved in 1pt/ 575mls water 1½ oz/40g flour	salt and pepper 5 carrots 1 onion

1. Fry the meat on both sides until browned.

2. Remove from the frying pan and place in a saucepan.

3. Chop the onions and carrots and fry lightly.

4. Remove from the frying pan and place with the meat in the saucepan.

5. Sprinkle the flour into the frying pan and stir well.

6. Add the stock cubes, water and seasoning. Continue stirring.

7. Add this to the meat and vegetables and cook gently over a low heat for 1-1½ hours until the meat is tender.

FRY CASSEROLE

Lamb Cutlet Casserole

INGREDIENTS		
1 dessertspoon oil 8 lamb cutlets 2 large onions peeled and sliced thickly into rings	5 potatoes, peeled and thinly sliced ½ pt/275mls vegetable stock 1 dessertspoon plain flour	2 dessertspoons worcestershire sauce 1 teaspoon dried mixed herbs (optional) salt and pepper

1. Pre-heat the oven to 160°C / 325°F / Gas Mark 3.

2. Partially cook the potatoes in boiling salted water for 5 minutes, then slice thinly.

3. Cook cutlets in a frying pan over a low heat for 5-10 mins until browned, turning once. Put on a warm plate.

4. Add the onions to the pan and cook gently for 2-3 minutes until browned.

6. Drain off all but 1 tablespoon of juice from the pan.

7. Scatter the flour in the pan and cook for 1 minute stirring constantly.

8. Add the stock, worcestershire sauce and mixed herbs. Cook until thickened. Add salt and pepper to taste.

9. To assemble: lightly grease a casserole dish. Lay half the potatoes on the base, then top with lamb cutlets. Pour over the thickened stock and onions. Lay the rest of the potatoes on top.

10. Cook in the oven for 45 minutes until cutlets are tender and the potatoes on the surface are golden.

COST HEALTHY

NUMBER OF SERVINGS

PREPARATION TIME	COOKING TIME
30 minutes	**45** minutes

UTENSILS NEEDED

FRYING PAN
CASSEROLE DISH

HANDY HINTS

Leftover potatoes could be used.

Pork chops could also be used.

31

FRY **OVEN**

COST	HEALTHY

NUMBER OF SERVINGS

PREPARATION TIME	COOKING TIME
20 minutes	**30** minutes

UTENSILS NEEDED

FRYING PAN
CASSEROLE DISH

HANDY HINTS

Place flour and seasoning in a small plastic bag. Place liver in the bag and shake well, coating the liver pieces.

Liver Hot-Pot

INGREDIENTS		
1lb/450g liver 1oz/25g flour salt and pepper 1/4 pt/150ml milk	1 dessertspoon cooking oil 2 onions 6 mushrooms	1/4 pt/150ml stock 2 dessertspoons tomato sauce 3 cooked potatoes

1. Pre-heat the oven to 190°C / 350°F / Gas Mark 5.

2. Wash the liver, dry with kitchen paper. Cut liver into small pieces.

3. Peel and chop onions, wash and slice mushrooms.

4. Season flour with salt and pepper. Coat liver on all sides with seasoned flour.

5. Heat the oil in pan and fry onions until tender.
   Add mushrooms and fry for a few minutes. Add liver and brown.

6. Gradually add in stock, milk and tomato sauce.
   Bring to the boil stirring continuously. Season well.

7. Pour into casserole dish. Cover with the sliced potato.

8. Bake in the pre-heated oven for approx. 30 minutes.

Pork Casserole

FRY **OVEN**

COST	HEALTHY

NUMBER OF SERVINGS

PREPARATION TIME	COOKING TIME
15 minutes	**1½** hours

UTENSILS NEEDED
FRYING PAN
CASSEROLE DISH

HANDY HINTS

This dish is delicious served with baked potatoes (page 97), boiled potatoes or boiled noodles and carrots or brocolli.

INGREDIENTS

1½ lbs/675g diced pork	1 teaspoon curry powder	pinch of mixed herbs
1 small green pepper	½ teaspoon salt	½ pt/275mls vegetable stock (1 vegetable stock cube mixed with ½ pt/275mls of warm water)
1 dessertspoon oil	½ teaspoon pepper	
1 onion peeled and chopped	1oz/50g flour	
6 mushrooms sliced	1 tin tomatoes	

1. Pre-heat the oven to 160°C / 325°F / Gas Mark 3.

2. Remove stalks and seeds from the pepper and chop it up.

3. Heat the oil and fry the onion, pepper and mushrooms for 3 minutes. Transfer to a casserole dish.

4. Add the curry powder, salt and pepper to the flour, and coat the pork in this mixture.

5. Fry the coated pork for 5 minutes and then put into the casserole dish with the vegetables. Add tomatoes, herbs and vegetable stock.

6. Cover tightly and cook in the pre-heated oven for 1½ hours.

COST	HEALTHY

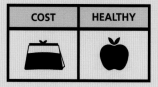

NUMBER OF SERVINGS

PREPARATION TIME	COOKING TIME
30 minutes	**15** minutes

UTENSILS NEEDED

FRYING PAN

HANDY HINTS

Chicken, beef or lamb can be used instead of pork. A variety of ingredients can be added to fried rice - chopped onion or garlic can be fried with the rice. Add spring onions, frozen peas, peeled prawns or diced cooked chicken halfway through cooking.

Pork Stir-Fry

INGREDIENTS		
1lb/450g pork pieces 1 clove garlic 1 onion 6 mushrooms 1 pepper	2 carrots 2 dessertspoons soy sauce 2 teaspoons cornflour 1 dessertspoon oil	1 chicken stock cube dissolved in $^1/_4$ pt/150mls of boiling water

① Cut pork into thin slices.

② Cut onions into thin slices and chop garlic.

③ Slice mushrooms and cut carrots and pepper into thin strips.

④ Mix the $^1/_4$ pt/150mls chicken stock with the soy sauce.

Blend in the cornflour and mix to a smooth paste.

⑤ Heat the oil in a large frying pan.

Add the pork and fry until well browned.

⑥ Add onion and carrot to the pan and fry for 2-3 minutes.

⑦ Then add mushrooms and pepper to pork mixture and continue frying for 2-3 minutes.

⑧ Pour the stock mixture into the pan and bring to the boil, stirring all the time. Simmer for 5 minutes.

Serve immediately with fried rice.

TO MAKE FRIED RICE:

Beat an egg in a cup. Fry in a little oil. Place on a plate and chop finely. Add the cooked rice to the frying pan. Mix in the chopped egg. Stir until well heated.

Stuffed Pork Chops in Foil

INGREDIENTS		
4 thick pork chops salt and pepper pinch of mixed herbs	6-8 mushrooms chopped 1 dessertspoon flour	1 dessertspoon lemon juice

1. Pre-heat the oven to 160°C / 325°F / Gas Mark 3.

2. Trim the chops and season on both sides with salt and pepper.

3. Fry chops in a little oil to seal in the juices. Remove from the pan.

4. Cook mushrooms for a few minutes until soft. Stir in lemon juice.

5. Sprinkle the flour and mixed herbs over mushrooms and cook for a few minutes. Remove from heat.

6. Cut four pieces of tin foil large enough to completely cover each chop.

7. Place a chop in the centre of each piece of foil.

8. Cover with the mushroom mixture.

9. Fold the foil over loosely and seal completely.

10. Place on a baking sheet and cook in a pre-heated oven for 35-40 minutes.

COST   HEALTHY

NUMBER OF SERVINGS

PREPARATION TIME   COOKING TIME

15 minutes   **40** minutes

UTENSILS NEEDED

FRYING PAN
CASSEROLE DISH

HANDY HINTS

This dish is delicious served with baked potatoes (page 97).

Onions can also be used with the mushrooms.

Fish

OVEN

Baked Stuffed Fish

INGREDIENTS		
8 small fillets of fish 2 ozs breadcrumbs (2 slices) 1 onion finely chopped salt and pepper	1 tablespoon finely chopped parsley (or 1 tablespoon dried parsley) or ¼ teaspoon mixed herbs	1 teaspoon of vegetable oil a little lemon juice (or grated rind)

COST	HEALTHY

NUMBER OF SERVINGS

PREPARATION TIME	COOKING TIME
20 minutes	**30** minutes

UTENSILS NEEDED

CASSEROLE DISH

HANDY HINTS

Fish suitable for baking: cod, haddock, mackerel, herrings, trout.

1. Pre-heat the oven to 180°C / 350°F / Gas Mark 4 .

2. Clean and prepare fish. Dry in kitchen paper.

3. Mix breadcrumbs, chopped onion, parsley/mixed herbs, salt and pepper, in a small bowl.

4. Heat oil and stir into crumb mixture.
Finally add a little lemon rind or juice.

5. Lay 4 fillets on a greased dish, skin side down and spoon stuffing carefully onto each fillet. Flatten well down and cover with the other four fillets. Cover with foil.

6. Bake for 20-30 minutes, depending on size and thickness of fish.

7. Lift fish carefully on to a warmed serving dish and surround with cooked peas, lemon wedges and parsley .

NUMBER OF SERVINGS

PREPARATION TIME	COOKING TIME
10 minutes	**10** minutes

UTENSILS NEEDED

DEEP FAT FRYER

Chip Shop Fish Supper

INGREDIENTS		
¼ pint (150ml) fritter batter (see recipe page 42)	2 dessertspoons flour salt and pepper 4 fillets white fish	

① Make the batter (page 42).

② Mix the flour, salt and pepper together.

Coat the fish with the seasoned flour.

③ Dip the fish in the batter and place in deep fat fryer for about 10 minutes according to thickness of the fish.

④ Drain on kitchen paper.

Crispy Baked Cod in Tomato Sauce

CASSEROLE

COST	HEALTHY

NUMBER OF SERVINGS

PREPARATION TIME	**COOKING TIME**
30 minutes	**30** minutes

INGREDIENTS		
1½ lb/675g cod or haddock (filleted and skinned)	**TOMATO SAUCE:** 1 small onion 1 clove garlic 1-2 celery sticks 1 tin tomatoes salt and pepper 1 level teaspoon sugar 1 teaspoon of vegetable oil	**TOPPING:** 1 teaspoon of vegetable oil 2oz/50g white or brown breadcrumbs (2 slices) 1oz/25g cheddar cheese grated

1. Pre-heat the oven to 200°C / 400°F / Gas Mark 6.
2. Wash and dry the fish, then cut into neat pieces.
   Place in a lightly greased shallow ovenproof dish.
3. TOMATO SAUCE:
   Heat oil in a small saucepan. Stir in the finely chopped onions, garlic and celery. Cook for 2-3 minutes until the vegetables soften but have not become coloured. Add the tomatoes, sugar, salt and pepper and bring to the boil, stirring all the time. Cover and simmer for 10-15 minutes, stirring occasionally.
4. Meanwhile prepare the topping. Heat oil in a small saucepan. Remove from the heat. Using a fork, stir in the breadcrumbs, then mix in the grated cheese.
5. Pour the tomato sauce over the fish. Sprinkle the topping evenly all over.
6. Cook for 30 minutes until the topping is crisp and brown.

UTENSILS NEEDED

SHALLOW OVEN DISH

HANDY HINTS

Fish suitable for baking: haddock, mackerel, herring, and trout.

BOIL/STEW

GRILL

COST	HEALTHY

NUMBER OF SERVINGS

PREPARATION TIME	COOKING TIME
30 minutes	**10** minutes

UTENSILS NEEDED

CASSEROLE DISH
SAUCEPAN

HANDY HINTS

Add 8oz/225g of frozen vegetable, to the fish before cooking for 10 minutes. (Point 2)

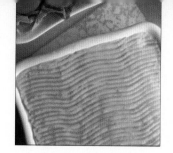

Family Fish Pie

INGREDIENTS		
1½ lb/675g filleted cod	few drops of lemon juice	1oz/25g margarine
1 onion finely chopped	¼ pt/150mls water	1 dessertspoon of flour
salt and pepper	½ pt/275mls milk	8 potatoes (cooked and mashed)

1. Skin the fish and cut into 4 pieces. Wash in cold water.

2. Place in a saucepan with onion and lemon juice.
   Add the water and milk. Cover and cook gently for 10 minutes.

3. Drain the fish, saving the stock.

4. Melt the margarine in a saucepan. Add the flour and cook for 2 minutes until it forms a soft ball. Remove from heat and add the fish stock gradually.
   Bring to the boil, reduce heat and cook for another 2 minutes.

5. Grease a pie dish and add a little sauce.
   Place fish in dish and cover with remaining sauce.

6. Using a piping bag with a rose nozzle, pipe the mashed potatoes around edge of dish or spoon the potatoes around the edge.

7. Brown under the grill or in the oven.

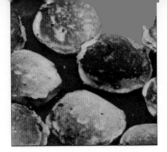

Fish Cakes

INGREDIENTS		
12oz/350g cooked white fish (cod or whiting) 6 potatoes mashed salt and pepper	1oz/25g melted butter 2 dessertspoons chopped parsley vegetable oil	2 beaten eggs 3oz/75g white breadcrumbs - (3 slices) 2 dessertspoons flour

1. Place the flaked fish, potatoes, butter, parsley, salt and pepper and 1 beaten egg in a bowl and mix gently with a fork.
   Place in the fridge for 30 minutes.

2. Roll into a long 'snake' on a floured surface.
   Cut into 8 portions and shape each into a flat round.

3. Dip the cakes into the second beaten egg and coat in breadcrumbs.

4. Fry or grill the fish cakes until golden brown on each side.

FRIDGE

FRY

COST

NUMBER OF SERVINGS

PREPARATION TIME	COOKING TIME
30 minutes	**15** minutes

UTENSILS NEEDED

FRYING PAN

HANDY HINTS

Tinned salmon may be used instead of white fish if preferred.

Use a plastic bag to hold breadcrumbs.

Fritter Batter

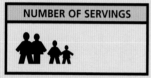
PREPARATION TIME	COOKING TIME
10 minutes	

UTENSILS NEEDED

MIXING BOWL

HANDY HINTS

This batter could be used for banana and pineapple fritters etc.

INGREDIENTS		
4oz/110g plain white flour 1 egg	½ teaspoon salt 1 teaspoon of breadsoda	¼ pt/150mls milk

1. Sieve the flour, salt and breadsoda into a bowl.

2. Make a well in the centre of the bowl, add the egg and a little of the milk.

3. Stir briskly, gradually adding the rest of the milk beating well all the time.

4. Leave in the fridge until ready to use.

Golden Cod

FRY

OVEN

INGREDIENTS		
1¹/₂ lbs/675g cod, cut into 6 pieces salt and pepper juice of a lemon 1 dessertspoon water	1 onion peeled and chopped 1 teaspoon vegetable oil 1 carrot peeled and grated	4oz/120g cheese grated 4 potatoes cooked peeled and sliced

1. Pre-heat the oven to 180°C / 350°F / Gas Mark 4.

2. Place fish in oven-proof dish, sprinkle with salt, pepper and juice of lemon. Add water.

3. Heat oil in a pan, fry onion and carrot for 2-3 minutes. Then spread over fish.

4. Put a layer of cooked potato slices on top of vegetables.

5. Bake in the pre-heated oven for 30 minutes or until fish is cooked.

6. After 20 minutes of cooking time, sprinkle with grated cheese.

COST

HEALTHY

NUMBER OF SERVINGS

PREPARATION TIME	COOKING TIME
30 minutes	**30** minutes

UTENSILS NEEDED

FRYING PAN
OVEN-PROOF DISH

HANDY HINTS

Any white fish may be used.

Breadcrumbs may be used instead of potatoes.

Salmon Surprise

INGREDIENTS		
1 packet of cream of mushroom soup 1 level dessertspoon flour	½ pt/275mls cold water 1 tin of peas 5 potatoes (boiled)	1 large tin of salmon 2oz/50g grated cheese salt and pepper a little milk

1 Empty contents of packet of soup into saucepan and add flour.
Gradually blend in the cold water and mix well.
Bring to the boil, stirring all the time.
Simmer for 5 minutes, stirring occasionally.

2 Empty tin of salmon, including juices into
soup mixture, add the strained peas and mix gently.
Pour mixture into a casserole dish.

3 Mash potatoes adding the milk, salt and pepper,
then pipe or spoon around salmon mixture.

4 Sprinkle salmon mixture with grated cheese and
brown lightly under a grill or bake in a pre-heated oven
180°C / 350°F / Gas Mark 4 for 20 minutes.

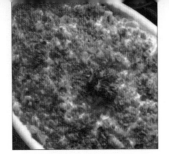

Tuna Quick Bake

INGREDIENTS		
2 cans tuna, drained (198g/7oz)	1 can of mushroom soup	salt and pepper
		knob of margarine
1 onion, chopped	1 teaspoon worcestershire sauce	8oz/225g fresh brown breadcrumbs (6 slices)

FISH SAUCE:

1. Pre-heated the oven to 180°C / 350°F / Gas Mark 4.

2. Flake the tuna and mix together with the onion, soup, worcestershire sauce, salt and pepper.

3. Pour some of the fish sauce into a casserole dish. Add a layer of breadcrumbs, followed by a layer of sauce.

4. Continue layering in this way until all the ingredients have been used up.

5. Finish with a layer of breadcrumbs on the top, dot the surface with the margarine and bake in the pre-heated oven for 20-25 minutes.

6. Serve immediately.

COST	HEALTHY

NUMBER OF SERVINGS

PREPARATION TIME	COOKING TIME
10 minutes	**25** minutes

UTENSILS NEEDED

CASSEROLE DISH

HANDY HINTS

Add a little grated cheese to the breadcrumbs for the top of the dish.

45

Chicken

American-Style Chicken

INGREDIENTS		
3ozs/75g corn flakes (crushed)	1 teaspoon mixed herbs	4 chicken legs
1 egg (beaten)	salt and pepper	

1. Pre-heat the oven to 190°C / 375°F / Gas Mark 5.

2. Mix the crushed corn flakes, salt, pepper and mixed herbs together in a bowl.

3. Beat the egg in a separate bowl.

4. Dip the chicken pieces in the egg and then in the seasoned cornflake crumbs, pressing on well.

5. Place in a casserole dish, lined with tin foil. Bake in the pre-heated oven for 1 hour or until chicken is cooked.

6. Serve hot or cold with salad.

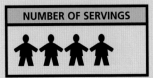

COST	HEALTHY

NUMBER OF SERVINGS

PREPARATION TIME	COOKING TIME
15 minutes	**60** minutes

UTENSILS NEEDED

CASSEROLE DISH

HANDY HINTS

Use a plastic bag to hold crushed cornflakes when coating the chicken.

OVEN

COST	HEALTHY
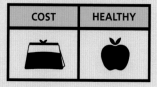	

NUMBER OF SERVINGS

PREPARATION TIME	COOKING TIME
15 minutes	**60** minutes

UTENSILS NEEDED

CASSEROLE DISH

HANDY HINTS

Serve with baked potato (page 97) or salad.

48

Chicken in Barbecue Sauce

INGREDIENTS		
8 chicken thighs/legs 2 medium onions thinly sliced ¹/₂ teaspoon salt	1 green pepper thinly sliced 6 dessertspoons tomato sauce	1 dessertspoon worcestershire sauce 1 teaspoon chilli powder

1. Pre-heat the oven to 190°C / 375°F / Gas Mark 5.

2. Mix all ingredients except the chicken to make the sauce.

3. Arrange the chicken in a single layer in the casserole dish.

4. Spoon over the sauce.

5. Cover and bake for 55-60 minutes, until the chicken is tender.

Chicken and Broccoli Pie

INGREDIENTS		
1 teaspoon vegetable oil	mushroom soup	salt and pepper
4 chicken fillets chopped	1lb/450g broccoli	2oz/50g white or brown breadcrumbs (2 slices)
1 onion	1 dessertspoon of curry powder	2oz/50g grated cheese
tin of chicken or	¼ pt/150mls milk	

1. Pre-heat the oven to 220°C / 425°F / Gas Mark 7.

2. Chop the onion finely and fry for 2-3 minutes.

3. Add the chicken pieces. Cook for 10 minutes.

4. Boil broccoli for 2-3 minutes.

5. Mix the milk, soup, curry powder salt and pepper together in a jug.

6. Put the cooked chicken pieces, onion and broccoli into the casserole dish.

7. Pour in the soup mixture and cover with the breadcrumbs and grated cheese.

8. Cook in the pre-heated oven for 30 minutes.

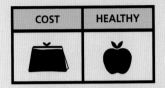

COST	HEALTHY

NUMBER OF SERVINGS

PREPARATION TIME	COOKING TIME
20 minutes	**30** minutes

UTENSILS NEEDED

FRYING PAN
CASSEROLE DISH

HANDY HINTS

Carrots or any other vegetable can be used instead of broccoli.

A cooked chicken could also be used.

OVEN **FRY**

NUMBER OF SERVINGS

PREPARATION TIME	COOKING TIME
20 minutes	**60** minutes

UTENSILS NEEDED

FRYING PAN
CASSEROLE DISH

Chicken Casserole - in a creamy sauce

INGREDIENTS		
6 chicken portions salt and pepper oil for frying 2ozs/50g margarine	³/₄ pt/425mls water 2 sticks celery scrubbed and chopped 1 packet broccoli and cauliflower soup	1 red pepper de-seeded and chopped

1. Pre-heat the oven to 200°C / 400°F / Gas Mark 6.

2. Season the chicken and fry slowly on both sides in the oil until golden brown.

3. Drain well and transfer to a casserole dish.

TO MAKE SAUCE:

4. Melt the margarine in a saucepan and fry the celery and red pepper gently until they soften, but do not colour.

5. Remove the pan from the heat, stir in the soup mix and then blend in the water. Bring to the boil, stirring all the time.

6. Simmer for 5 minutes.

7. Pour over the chicken pieces and cook on the middle shelf of a pre-heated oven for 55-60 minutes until light golden brown.

hicken Casserole with Tomatoes

FRY   OVEN

COST	HEALTHY

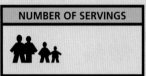

NUMBER OF SERVINGS

PREPARATION TIME	COOKING TIME
40 minutes	**1½** hours

UTENSILS NEEDED
FRYING PAN
CASSEROLE DISH

HANDY HINTS
Not all vegetables here need to be used. Select according to availability, choice and cost.

INGREDIENTS

8 chicken portions	pinch of chilli powder	1 chicken stock cube dissolved in ½ pt/275mls of boiling water
2 teaspoons oil	1 teaspoon mixed herbs	
4 carrots (peeled and sliced)	1 can tomatoes	chopped fresh parsley to garnish (optional)
4 celery sticks trimmed and sliced	salt and pepper	
	1 medium onion	

1. Pre-heat the oven to 190°C / 375°F / Gas Mark 5.

2. Heat the oil in a pan and brown half the chicken pieces thoroughly on all sides. This will take about 10 minutes. Remove with a spoon, then fry the remaining pieces. Remove and set aside.

3. Fry the onion, carrots and celery over a medium heat for 10 minutes, stirring occasionally, until soft but not brown. Stir in the chilli powder, herbs, tomatoes and stock.

4. Return the chicken to the pan, season to taste and bring to the boil. Place in a casserole dish.

5. Cover and cook in the centre of the oven for 1 hour.

6. Remove the lid and continue cooking for a further 15-30 minutes until the meat is very tender.

7. To serve: Sprinkle with the chopped fresh parsley.

OVEN | **FRY**

COST	HEALTHY

NUMBER OF SERVINGS

PREPARATION TIME	COOKING TIME
30 minutes	**30** minutes

UTENSILS NEEDED

FRYING PAN
CASSEROLE DISH

HANDY HINTS

Boil 4 chicken legs and remove the meat from the bone instead of using 1 cooked chicken.

Fresh chicken fillets can be used. Fry gently before adding vegetables.

Chicken Curry

INGREDIENTS		
1 cooked chicken	1 onion	1 teaspoon vegetable oil
5 mushrooms	1 clove of garlic	1 chicken stock cube
1 pepper	2 dessertspoons medium curry powder	1 dessertspoon flour

1. Remove the chicken off the bone.

2. Slice mushrooms, peppers, onion and garlic.

3. Dissolve the stock cube in $^1/_2$ pt/275mls of boiling water.

4. Heat the oil in a frying pan and gently fry the onions and garlic.

5. Add mushrooms and pepper to the frying pan and cook for 2 to 3 minutes.

6. Add curry powder and flour to the pan and cook for one minute stirring all the time.

7. Stir in the stock and chicken pieces.

8. Reduce heat, cook slowly for 10 minutes without stirring.

9. Serve with boiled rice.

Chicken Hot-Pot

FRY

OVEN

COST	HEALTHY

INGREDIENTS		
1 teaspoon veg. oil	4 large potatoes peeled and cut into large slices	2 chicken stock cubes dissolved in 1pt/575ml of boiling water
4 chicken leg pieces or breasts	1 small green pepper, chopped (optional)	salt and pepper
1 large onion, thinly sliced	3 large tomatoes peeled and chopped or 1 tin of tomatoes	2 sticks celery, sliced
8oz/225g frozen sweetcorn or peas		

NUMBER OF SERVINGS

PREPARATION TIME 20 minutes

COOKING TIME 65 minutes

1. Pre-heat the oven to 180°C / 350°F / Gas Mark 4.

2. Heat the oil in the frying pan, add the chicken and cook until brown on all sides.

3. Place chicken in a casserole dish.

4. Add onion, salt, pepper, celery and potatoes to the juices in the frying pan and cook for 5 minutes. Drain off the fat.

5. Add the tomatoes and stock. Bring to the boil.

6. Pour this over chicken pieces in the casserole dish.

7. Cover and cook for 45 to 50 minutes.

8. Add sweetcorn and/or peas and cook for another 15 minutes.

UTENSILS NEEDED
FRYING PAN
CASSEROLE DISH

HANDY HINTS

Use a variety of vegetables. These may be cooked in a saucepan on the top of the cooker.

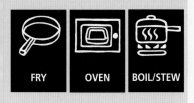

FRY | OVEN | BOIL/STEW

COST	HEALTHY

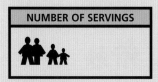

NUMBER OF SERVINGS

PREPARATION TIME	COOKING TIME
20 minutes	**60** minutes

UTENSILS NEEDED

FRYING PAN
CASSEROLE DISH

HANDY HINTS

A tin of chicken or mushroom soup can be used instead of the sauce.

54

Chicken in Mushroom Sauce

INGREDIENTS		
6 chicken portions	1 dessertspoon oil	6 mushrooms (sliced)
salt and pepper	SAUCE:	1 packet chicken soup
1 chicken stock cube dissolved in 6 dessert-spoons of water	1 dessertspoon vegetable oil	1 level teaspoon flour $^3/_4$ pt/425ml water

① Trim chicken joints and remove all fat and skin, then season with salt and pepper.

② Heat the oil in a large pan and fry the chicken portions on each side until golden brown.

③ Transfer the chicken portions to a casserole dish.

④ Pour the stock into the pan and stir, using a wooden spoon. Mix any crispy pieces from the sides of the pan. Boil for a few minutes. Keep for sauce.

TO MAKE SAUCE:

① Heat the oil in a saucepan, add the mushrooms and cook over a low heat until the mushrooms soften.

② Stir in the soup mix and the flour, then blend in the water.

③ Bring to the boil and simmer for 5 minutes.

④ Stir in the juices from the frying pan.

⑤ Pour the sauce over the chicken joints.

⑥ Cook in a pre-heated oven 190°C / 375°F / Gas Mark 5 for 50-60 minutes until the chicken is fully cooked.

FRY   OVEN

hicken, Mustard & Bacon Casserole

COST   HEALTHY

INGREDIENTS		
8 chicken portions skinned	1 dessertspoon mustard powder	2 dessertspoons lemon juice
8 back rashers trimmed	3 dessertspoons plain flour	2 chicken stock cubes (dissolve in 1pt/575ml of boiling water)
salt and pepper		

NUMBER OF SERVINGS

PREPARATION TIME	COOKING TIME
15 minutes	**1½** hours

UTENSILS NEEDED

LARGE FRYING PAN
CASSEROLE DISH

(1) Pre-heat the oven to 190°C / 375°F / Gas Mark 5.

(2) Wrap the chicken pieces in the bacon rashers and secure each one with a cocktail stick.

(3) Cook until brown on all sides in a dry pan.

(4) Remove from the pan with a spoon and put to one side.

(5) Add the mustard powder, flour, salt and pepper into the pan and cook, stirring for 1 minute.

(6) Add the stock and the lemon juice and bring to the boil stirring continuously.

(7) Place the chicken pieces in a casserole dish, add the stock from the frying pan and cover. Cook in pre-heated oven for 1-1½ hours.

FRY

BOIL/STEW

COST	HEALTHY
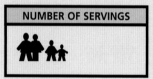	

NUMBER OF SERVINGS

PREPARATION TIME	COOKING TIME
30 minutes	**30** minutes

UTENSILS NEEDED

FRYING PAN
SAUCEPAN

HANDY HINTS

Stir frequently to prevent the risotto from sticking to the bottom of the pan.

Chicken Risotto

INGREDIENTS		
10oz/280g long grain rice 1 onion 1 clove of garlic 1 green or red pepper	1 teaspoon oil 5 mushrooms 1 small packet (or 1 small tin) of frozen corn	salt and pepper 3 or 4 chicken fillets 1 chicken stock cube dissolved in 3/4 pt /425ml of boiling water

1. Boil rice for approx. 5 mins, and drain.
2. Chop onion, pepper and mushrooms.
3. Cut chicken fillets into cubes.
4. Crush the garlic or chop into fine pieces.
5. Fry chicken pieces in vegetable oil.
6. Add garlic, onions, peppers and mushrooms. Fry gently.
7. Add rice to pan.
8. Stir in stock, add corn, salt and pepper.
9. Bring to boil and cook gently for 30 minutes, or until all the liquid has been absorbed.
10. Season to taste.

Chicken & Vegetable Casserole

INGREDIENTS		
4 chicken portions 3 large carrots 2 onions 6 mushrooms	½ pt/275ml chicken stock or (2 stock cubes dissolved in ½ pt/275ml boiling water)	2 dessertspoons lemon juice ½ dessertspoon mixed herbs salt and pepper

1. Pre-heat the oven to 180°C / 350°F / Gas Mark 4.

2. Wash, peel and chop carrots, onion and mushrooms.

3. Place chicken portions in a casserole dish with carrots, onion and mushrooms.

4. Pour in chicken stock, lemon juice, mixed herbs, salt and pepper.

5. Bake for 1-1½ hours or until chicken is cooked.

6. Serve with baked potatoes (page 97).

COST

HEALTHY

NUMBER OF SERVINGS

PREPARATION TIME
15 minutes

COOKING TIME
1½ hours

UTENSILS NEEDED

CASSEROLE DISH

HANDY HINTS

This is a basic recipe for a tasty casserole. Any vegetables can be used instead of mushrooms and carrots.
Use vegetables in season.

Vegetarian

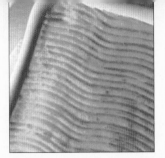

Cheese, Onion & Potato Pie

BOIL/STEW

OVEN

INGREDIENTS		
8 large potatoes	4oz/100g grated cheese	
1 onion, grated	salt and pepper	

① Pre-heat the oven to 200°C / 400°F / Gas Mark 6.

② Boil the potatoes, strain and mash.

③ Add onion, grated cheese, salt and pepper to the potatoes.

④ Place in a casserole dish.

⑤ Put under the grill for a few minutes to form a crust on the potato, or bake in a pre-heated oven for 20 minutes.

COST	HEALTHY

NUMBER OF SERVINGS

PREPARATION TIME	COOKING TIME
15 minutes	**20** minutes

UTENSILS NEEDED

CASSEROLE DISH
SAUCEPAN

HANDY HINTS

Serve with baked beans or salad.

FRY **OVEN**

COST	HEALTHY

NUMBER OF SERVINGS

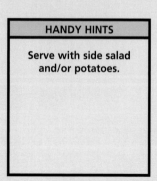

PREPARATION TIME	COOKING TIME
20 minutes	**20** minutes

UTENSILS NEEDED

CASSEROLE DISH
FRYING PAN

HANDY HINTS

Serve with side salad
and/or potatoes.

Mushroom Bake

INGREDIENTS		
16 mushrooms, sliced	1 red and 1 green pepper, chopped	TOPPING:
8oz/225g breadcrumbs	2 onions, chopped	2oz/50g grated cheese
6oz/180g cheese grated	a little cooking oil	2oz/50g breadcrumbs

1. Pre-heat the oven to 180°C / 350°F / Gas Mark 4.

2. Heat the oil in the frying pan.

3. Add the onions and peppers and cook for 5 minutes. Keep covered during cooking.

4. Add mushrooms. Cook for another 5 minutes, with the lid on.

5. Add 6oz/180g of breadcrumbs and 4oz/110g cheese.

6. Mix well together and place in casserole dish.

7. Top with grated cheese and breadcrumbs mixed together.

8. Bake in a pre-heated oven for 20 minutes.

Spanish Omelette

FRY

GRILL

INGREDIENTS		
1 dessertspoon vegetable oil 2 onions, chopped 1 red pepper, cored and chopped	salt and pepper 4 eggs 2 large potatoes boiled and chopped	1 dessertspoon chopped parsley

COST	HEALTHY

NUMBER OF SERVINGS

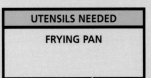

PREPARATION TIME	COOKING TIME
10 minutes	**15** minutes

UTENSILS NEEDED

FRYING PAN

HANDY HINTS

A good way of using leftover potato.

Serve with salad.

1. Heat 1 dessertspoon of oil in a frying pan.

2. Add the onions and cook until soft.

3. Add the red pepper, cook for 5 minutes.

4. Beat the eggs in a bowl. Add salt and pepper.

5. Stir the potatoes, parsley and fried vegetables into the egg mixture.

6. Pour the egg mixture into the heated frying pan and spread evenly to the edge.

7. Cook for 5 minutes until the egg mixture comes away from the side of the pan.

8. Place the pan under a pre-heated moderate grill for about 3 minutes to cook the top of the omelette.

COST	HEALTHY

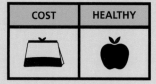

NUMBER OF SERVINGS

PREPARATION TIME	COOKING TIME
15 minutes	**20** minutes

UTENSILS NEEDED

FRYING PAN

HANDY HINTS

A little soya sauce can be added for extra flavour.

Sweet and sour sauce can also be used.

Stir-Fry Vegetables

INGREDIENTS		
1 green pepper 1 yellow pepper 10 mushrooms 1 onion	1 dessertspoon oil 1/4 pt/150ml stock (1 stock cube dissolved in water)	salt and pepper 3 carrots peas / beans

1. Peel and slice the carrots.

2. Slice the peppers, onion and mushrooms thinly.

3. Heat the oil in a frying pan. Add the mixed vegetables and stir well.

4. Add the stock. Keep stirring.

5. Cover the vegetables and cook gently for 10-15 minutes, until the vegetables are tender but still crisp. Add the peas /beans and cook for a further 3-5 minutes.

6. Serve with boiled rice, pasta or potatoes.

Veggie Burger

INGREDIENTS		
1 leek or onion, finely chopped	2 dessertspoons chopped parsley	wholemeal breadcrumbs
1 clove garlic, crushed	5 potatoes, cooked and mashed	1 dessertspoon of vegetable oil
5 mushrooms, chopped		
1 carrot finely, chopped	salt and pepper	

COST   **HEALTHY**

NUMBER OF SERVINGS

1. Heat the vegetable oil, add the onion and/or leek and fry until softened.

2. Add mushrooms, carrot and garlic and fry for 5 minutes.

3. Strain off any liquid.

4. Add vegetables and parsley to the mashed potato.

5. Season with salt and pepper.

6. Divide mixture into 8 portions and shape into rounds.

7. Coat with breadcrumbs. Grill or fry for two minutes on both sides until golden.

PREPARATION TIME	COOKING TIME
15 minutes	**5** minutes

UTENSILS NEEDED

FRYING PAN

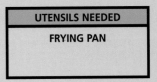

HANDY HINTS

Serve with a crunchy mixed salad.

OVEN

COST	HEALTHY

NUMBER OF SERVINGS

PREPARATION TIME	COOKING TIME
20 minutes	**1½** hours

UTENSILS NEEDED

CASSEROLE DISH

HANDY HINTS

Instead of a vegetable stock cube cook the vegetables for 1hr in salted water, drain and add 1pt /575mls of white sauce (page 13). Sprinkle with breadcrumbs and cheese and return to the oven for 30 mins.

Vegetarian Casserole

INGREDIENTS		
2lbs/900g vegetable mix: potatoes carrots onions	turnips peas lentils, etc.	salt and pepper 1pt/575mls vegetable stock (2 vegetable stock cubes)

1. Pre-heat the oven to 190°C / 375°F / Gas Mark 5.

2. Slice potatoes and put a layer in the bottom of the casserole dish.

3. Layer vegetables etc., over the potatoes.

4. Repeat layering until the dish is full. Season between the layers.

5. Finish with a layer of potatoes.

6. Add vegetable stock.

7. Cover and cook in the pre-heated oven for 1½ hours.

Vegetable Curry

FRY

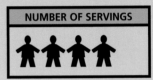
INGREDIENTS

1 dessertspoon vegetable oil	salt and pepper	1 dessertspoon coconut
1 chopped onion	1pt/575ml stock (2 stock cubes dissolved in 1pt/575ml boiling water)	2ozs/50g sultanas
1 or 2 apples, cored and peeled		1 teaspoon brown sugar
2 dessertspoons curry powder		1 teaspoon lemon juice
	2lbs/900g mixed vegetables (mushrooms, carrots celery etc.)	1 tin peas/beans
1 dessertspoon flour		1 dessertspoon chutney (optional)

NUMBER OF SERVINGS

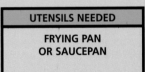

PREPARATION TIME	COOKING TIME
30 minutes	**45** minutes

1. Prepare the mixture of vegetables. Wash them and chop into cubes. Place in a saucepan.

2. Add the apple, lentils, lemon juice, coconut, sultanas, brown sugar and chutney. Add ³/₄ pt/425ml of stock and boil for 20 mins.

3. Heat the oil and fry the onion until it is soft.

4. Stir in the curry powder, flour and remainder of stock.

5. Bring to the boil. Add this to the mixed vegetables and season.

6. Simmer for 10 minutes. Reduce heat and cook slowly for another 20 minutes.

UTENSILS NEEDED

FRYING PAN
OR SAUCEPAN

HANDY HINTS

Serve with rice or pasta.

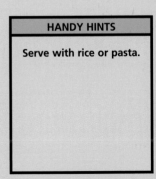

OVEN

COST	HEALTHY
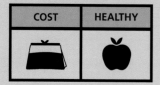	

NUMBER OF SERVINGS

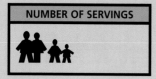

PREPARATION TIME	COOKING TIME
40 minutes	**40** minutes

UTENSILS NEEDED

CASSEROLE DISH

Vegetable Goulash

INGREDIENTS		
2lb/900g mixed vegetables i.e., carrots, potatoes, mushrooms, corn, courgettes, etc.	1 clove of garlic, finely chopped	1 red and green pepper
	1 dessertspoon cooking oil	4 dessertspoons tomato puree
2 onions, finely chopped	14oz/400g can of chopped tomatoes	2 dessertspoons paprika
		salt and pepper

1. Pre-heat the oven to 190°C / 375°F / Gas Mark 5.

2. Cut the vegetables into bite-sized pieces.

3. Heat the oil and fry the onions and garlic in the oil for 5 minutes.

4. Mix in the chopped vegetables, tomatoes, tomato puree, paprika and seasoning. Fry for another 5 minutes.

5. Transfer to a casserole dish. Bake in the oven until the vegetables are cooked for about 40 minutes.

Vegetable Lasagne

FRY

OVEN

COST | HEALTHY

NUMBER OF SERVINGS

PREPARATION TIME	COOKING TIME
30 minutes	**25** minutes

INGREDIENTS

1 large onion, sliced	1 can tomatoes	salt and pepper
1 green pepper, sliced	2 dessertspoons tomato sauce	½ pt/275ml vegetable stock
1 yellow pepper, sliced	8oz/225g lasagne or medium box of easi - cook lasagne	½ pt/275ml white sauce (page 12)
10 mushrooms, sliced		mixed herbs
3 carrots, finely chopped	grated cheddar cheese	
1 can kidney beans		

(1) Pre-heat the oven to 200°C / 400°F / Gas Mark 6.

(2) Fry the onions, peppers, mushrooms and carrots for 3-5 mins.

(3) Add the tomato sauce, kidney beans, tomatoes and vegetable stock. Season with salt and pepper.

(4) Layer the sheets of lasagne and vegetables in a casserole dish: starting with a layer of vegetables and finishing with a layer of lasagne.

(5) Make the white sauce (see sauces page 13) and pour on top.

(6) Sprinkle with mixed herbs and grated cheddar cheese.

(7) Bake in the pre-heated oven for 20 to 25 minutes.

UTENSILS NEEDED
**FRYING PAN
CASSEROLE DISH
SAUCEPAN**

HANDY HINTS

Serve with crunchy side salad or garlic bread.

GARLIC BREAD
Slice a french loaf in thick slices (do not cut through). Mix soft margarine/butter with crushed garlic. Spread on each slice of the loaf. Roll in tin foil and heat in a moderate oven for 10 minutes.

FRY **CASSEROLE**

COST	HEALTHY
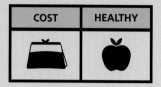	

NUMBER OF SERVINGS

PREPARATION TIME	COOKING TIME
30 minutes	**15** minutes

UTENSILS NEEDED

FRYING PAN
CASSEROLE DISH

HANDY HINTS

Try different shapes and colours of pasta for variety.

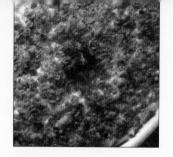

Vegetable Pasta Bake

INGREDIENTS		
1 dessertspoon vegetable oil	2 desssertspoons tomato sauce	1 pt/575ml cheese sauce (page 13)
1 onion, chopped	1 or 2 cloves of garlic	3 dessertspoons wholemeal breadcrumbs
1 green pepper, sliced	mixed herbs	
8 mushrooms, sliced	pepper	
1 tin tomatoes	200g/8oz pasta	

1. Pre-heat the oven to 200°C / 400°F / Gas Mark 6.

2. Heat the oil, fry the onion, pepper, mushrooms and crushed garlic for 5 minutes.

3. Add the tomatoes, tomatoe sauce, mixed herbs and a little pepper.

4. Bring to the boil, reduce heat and simmer for 20 minutes.

5. Cook the pasta in boiling water for 12-15 minutes until it is soft. Drain the pasta and add to the vegetable mix.

6. Stir and cook gently for 2-3 minutes.

7. Put the pasta and vegetable mix into and a casserole dish and cover with a thick cheese sauce. (page 13).

8. Sprinkle with grated cheese and breadcrumbs.

9. Bake in the pre-heated oven for 10-15 minutes.

Vegetable Risotto

BOIL/STEW

FRY

COST	HEALTHY

NUMBER OF SERVINGS

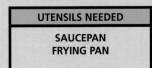

PREPARATION TIME	COOKING TIME
20 minutes	**20** minutes

INGREDIENTS		
10oz/280g rice $\frac{1}{2}$ pt/275ml stock (2 vegetable stock cubes dissolved in $\frac{1}{2}$ pt/275ml boiling water)	cooking oil $\frac{1}{2}$ lb/225g bag of frozen peas 6 mushrooms, chopped 1 finely chopped onion	1 can of kidney beans 1 green pepper, finely chopped 1lb/450g tin tomatoes

UTENSILS NEEDED

SAUCEPAN
FRYING PAN

1. Rinse rice and cook in stock for 10 minutes.

2. Heat the oil. Fry the chopped onion, mushrooms and pepper in the oil for 5 minutes.

3. Add the frozen peas, kidney beans and tomatoes to the fried vegetables and heat gently.

4. Stir in the rice and cook for 10 minutes until the liquid has been absorbed.

5. Serve with garlic bread and side salad.

Cakes

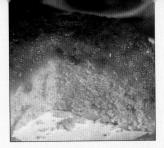

Apple Cake

INGREDIENTS		
8oz/225g flour	2 cooking apples	a little salt
3oz/85g margarine	1 egg, beaten	
4oz/110g sugar	a little milk	

1. Pre-heat the oven to 190°C / 375°F / Gas Mark 6.

2. Sieve flour and salt into a bowl.

3. Rub in margarine until the mixture looks like breadcrumbs.

4. Peel and chop the apples and add to the flour mixture. Add the sugar and mix well. Add the beaten egg.

5. If mixture is too dry, add a little milk to make a stiff dough.

6. Put the mixture into a greased sandwich tin and sprinkle with granulated sugar.

7. Bake in the pre-heated oven for about 40 minutes until golden brown.

OVEN

COST	HEALTHY

NUMBER OF SERVINGS

PREPARATION TIME	COOKING TIME
20 minutes	**40** minutes

UTENSILS NEEDED

SANDWICH TIN

HANDY HINTS

Fresh pears can be used.

Add a few sultanas for variety.

Serve hot or cold.

 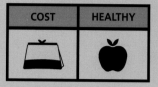
Apple (Rhubarb) Crumble

NUMBER OF SERVINGS

PREPARATION TIME	COOKING TIME
15 minutes	**30** minutes

UTENSILS NEEDED

PIE DISH
BOWL

INGREDIENTS		
3 cooking apples or 6 stalks of rhubarb 2oz/50g sugar 3 dessertspoons water	TOPPING: 6oz/180g flour 2oz/50g caster sugar	2oz/50g margarine

① Pre-heat the oven to 180°C / 350°F / Gas Mark 4.

② Put sliced apples (rhubarb), sugar and water in a saucepan and cook gently until they are soft. Place cooked fruit mixture in a pie dish.

③ Sieve flour into a bowl. Rub in margarine. Add sugar and mix thoroughly.

④ Sprinkle crumble mixture over fruit mixture.

⑤ Bake in the pre-heated oven for 30 minutes.

HANDY HINTS

Rhubarb can be used.

Ground or chopped almonds can be added to the crumble mixture for added flavour.

Fresh or tinned pears can also be used.

72

Apple (Rhubarb) Tart

OVEN

INGREDIENTS		
PASTRY INGREDIENTS:	**FILLING:**	
12oz/340g plain flour	2 or 3 medium cooking apples (4 stalks of rhubarb)	
6oz/180g hard margarine	2 oz sugar	
a little milk or water		

COST

① Pre-heat the oven to 220°C / 425°F / Gas Mark 7.

② Sieve the flour and salt into a baking bowl.
Cut the margarine and rub into flour with fingertips until the mixture resembles fine bread crumbs.

③ Add the water or milk to the flour mixture and mix to a stiff dough.

④ Divide the pastry in to $^1/_3$ and $^2/_3$ portions.

⑤ Roll the larger piece ($^2/_3$) into a circle and use to line the base of a large greased plate/pie dish. Slice apples (rhubarb) and arrange on the base of the plate. Sprinkle with sugar.

⑥ Roll out the second piece ($^1/_3$) of pastry to cover tart.
Wet edges of pastry and press the pastry top in place.

⑦ Bake in the pre-heated oven for 30 minutes.

NUMBER OF SERVINGS

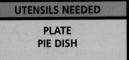

PREPARATION TIME	COOKING TIME
10 minutes	**30** minutes

UTENSILS NEEDED
PLATE
PIE DISH

HANDY HINTS

This pastry can be used for mince pies. Just add 2oz of caster sugar to the flour before rubbing in the margarine.

Cloves may be added to the apple.

OVEN

COST	HEALTHY
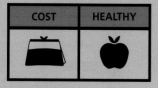	

NUMBER OF SERVINGS

PREPARATION TIME	COOKING TIME
10 minutes	**1½** hours

UTENSILS NEEDED

LOAF TIN

HANDY HINTS

Serve with hot custard.

Banana Bread

INGREDIENTS		
10oz/280g self-raising flour	½ teaspoon baking powder	½ teaspoon cinnamon
5oz/140g brown sugar	4oz/110g walnuts chopped	½ teaspoon nutmeg
3 eggs, beaten		7oz/200g melted margarine
3 bananas, mashed		

1 Pre-heat the oven to 180°C / 350°F / Gas Mark 4.

2 Mix the dry ingredients in one bowl.

3 Mix the wet ingredients in another bowl.

4 Mix the wet mixture and the dry mixture together.

5 Put into well greased loaf tin.

6 Bake in the pre-heated oven for 1½ hours.

Bread and Butter Pudding

OVEN

INGREDIENTS		
6 slices of bread 2oz/50g butter 1 egg	a little milk sugar sultanas	pinch of nutmeg

1. Pre-heat the oven to 190°C / 375°F / Gas Mark 5.

2. Cut crusts off the bread,(if preferred) butter it and cut into fingers.

3. Grease the dish. Then put a layer of bread fingers on the base of the dish. Sprinkle with sultanas and sugar.
Continue the layers, finishing with a layer of bread.

4. Beat egg and milk together and pour over the bread.

5. Sprinkle nutmeg on top.

6. Bake in the pre-heated oven for 30 minutes.

COST	HEALTHY

NUMBER OF SERVINGS

PREPARATION TIME	COOKING TIME
10 minutes	**30** minutes

UTENSILS NEEDED

PIE DISH

HANDY HINTS

A good way of using up stale bread.

Stale cake or scone crumbs may also be used.

Serve with hot custard.

OVEN

COST

NUMBER OF SERVINGS

PREPARATION TIME	COOKING TIME
20 minutes	**50** minutes

UTENSILS NEEDED

8" CAKE TIN

HANDY HINTS

Sultanas can be added to the cake mixture.

The cake maybe iced with a butter icing.

Carrot Cake

INGREDIENTS		
8ozs/225g caster sugar ¹/₂ cup cooking oil	8oz/225g grated carrots, raw 2 eggs	9oz/250g white self-raising flour

1. Pre-heat the oven to 190°C / 375°F / Gas Mark 4.

2. Mix sugar, grated carrots, eggs and oil together. Fold in flour and mix well.

3. Turn into an 8" round tin lined with greaseproof paper, and bake in the pre-heated oven.

4. Check after 50 minutes, by which time the centre of the cake should have risen.

5. Place on a wire tray to cool, with the greaseproof paper removed.

Cheese Cake

INGREDIENTS

1 pkt. digestive biscuits (9ozs/250g)	¼ pt/150ml cream	2ozs/50g low-fat margarine
tub of creamed cheese (5ozs/140g)	1 packet of lemon jelly	1 cup of water
	1 lemon	

BASE

Melt the margarine over a low heat and add the crushed biscuits and mix well. Press the mixture into a loose-bottomed 9" cake tin and place in the fridge.

FILLING

1 Melt the jelly in 1 cup of water. Allow to cool but not set.

2 Add the juice of the lemon and the lemon rind to the jelly.

3 Whisk together the cream cheese and cream.

4 Add this mixture to the jelly and blend well together.

5 Pour on top of the biscuit base.
    Place in fridge until it is firm and set.

OVEN

COST

NUMBER OF SERVINGS

PREPARATION TIME	COOKING TIME
45 minutes	**5-6** hours

UTENSILS NEEDED

A DEEP 10"/25CM ROUND CAKE TIN OR A DEEP 9"/23CM SQUARE TIN

HANDY HINTS

The whiskey may be poured over the prepared fruit and left overnight. Alternatively, the whiskey could be poured evenly over the cake about 30-40 minutes after it is removed from the oven, while the cake is still warm. To do this, first make a few holes in the top, with a fine skewer or darning needle.

Christmas Cake All-In-One

INGREDIENTS		
12oz/340g margarine	grated apple	4oz/110g cherries, washed, dried and halved
12oz/340g dark brown sugar	1lb currants	
7 eggs (Size 1)	12oz/340g sultanas	14oz/400g plain white flour
3 tablespoons whiskey	12oz/340g raisins	1½ teaspoon mixed spice
grated rind of 1 lemon	4oz/110g chopped almonds	1 teaspoon ground nutmeg
grated rind of 1 orange	4oz/110g mixed peel	4oz/110g ground almonds

1. Pre-heat the oven to 140°C / 275°F / Gas Mark 1.

2. Prepare the tin. For the bottom of the tin: cut either circles or squares of double-thickness greaseproof paper. For the sides: Cut a strip of double greaseproof paper about 1 inch higher than the depth of the tin. (Grease well).

3. Weigh all the ingredients carefully.

4. Place all the cake ingredients together in a very large mixing bowl or basin and beat with a wooden spoon until well mixed (4-6 minutes).

5. Place this mixture in the prepared tin and smooth the top with the back of a wet dessertspoon.

6. Bake in the pre-heated oven on the middle shelf for approx 5-6 hours. Check at intervals after 2½ hours as ovens tend to vary. Cover the cake with double greaseproof paper or foil for about the last 1-2 hours, to prevent the top of the cake from becoming too brown.

7. Test the cake carefully before removing it from the oven.

8. Leave the cake to cool in the tin overnight. Turn out and remove papers, then store.

Christmas Pudding

COST

INGREDIENTS

3oz/85 g self-raising flour	4oz/110g margarine melted and cooled	**MIX TOGETHER:**
½ level teaspoon mixed spice	grated apple	2 large eggs
½ level teaspoon ground nutmeg	8oz/225g currants	1 dessertspoon brandy/rum/whiskey
½ level teaspoon ground cinnamon	4oz/110g raisins	¼ pint/150ml guinness
4oz/110g white breadcrumbs	4oz/110g sultanas	juice and grated rind of 1 orange
6oz/150g dark brown sugar	2oz/50g cut mixed peel	juice and grated rind of 1 lemon
	2oz/50g cherries, halved, washed and dried	
	1oz/25g chopped almonds	

PREPARATION:

Have ready 1 greased 2 pint/1.1 litre pudding bowl. Cut a large circle of double greaseproof paper for the top of the pudding and grease well. Cut a large circle of tin foil, place over the double circle of greaseproof paper on top of the pudding.

TO MAKE PUDDING:

1. Sieve the flour and spices into a large bowl.

2. Add the breadcrumbs, sugar, prepared fruit, nuts, orange and lemon rind, make sure the rind is finely grated. Then mix thoroughly.

3. Make a well in the centre. Pour in the melted margarine, beaten eggs, spirits and guinness mixture. Mix thoroughly with a wooden spoon.

4. Cover and leave to stand overnight. The mixture is slack in the beginning but thickens overnight. Mix well again before filling the bowl.

5. Place the pudding bowl in a saucepan of water and boil for 2-3 hours. Keep the water topped up in the saucepan.

NUMBER OF SERVINGS

PREPARATION TIME	COOKING TIME
45 minutes	**2-3** hours

UTENSILS NEEDED

2 PT PUDDING BOWL
LARGE POT

HANDY HINTS

Stand overnight.

OVEN

COST

NUMBER OF SERVINGS

PREPARATION TIME
30
minutes

COOKING TIME
35
minutes

UTENSILS NEEDED

2 x 6 ½ or 7 ½ inch (16 or 19 cm) sandwich tins.

HANDY HINTS

Ideal for birthday cakes.

To make a chocolate cake substitute 4 oz flour and 2oz drinking chocolate for 6oz flour. (Omit coffee essence).

Grease tins and put circle of greaseproof paper at base of each tin.

Coffee Cake

INGREDIENTS		
6oz/180g margarine (at room temp.)	6oz/180g self-raising flour, sieved	COFFEE ICING:
6oz/180g caster sugar	1 dessertspoon coffee essence	8oz/225g icing sugar
3 large eggs		1 teaspoon coffee essence
		1 dessertspoon milk

1   Pre-heat the oven to 180°C / 350°F / Gas Mark 4.

ALL-IN-ONE METHOD

1   Place all the ingredients for the cake in a mixing bowl and beat with a wooden spoon until well mixed (2-3 minutes).
Place half the mixture in each of the prepared tins.
Bake in the pre-heated oven for 25-35 minutes.
When cooked remove from tins and allow to cool on a wire tray.

TO MAKE ICING

1   Place all the ingredients together in a mixing bowl and beat with a wooden spoon until smooth.

TO FINISH CAKE

1   Sandwich the two cakes with a little of the icing.

2   Pipe the remaining icing on top of the cake.

80

Eve's Pudding

BOIL/STEW

OVEN

COST	HEALTHY
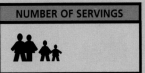	

NUMBER OF SERVINGS

PREPARATION TIME	COOKING TIME
20 minutes	**60** minutes

UTENSILS NEEDED
PYREX DISH

HANDY HINTS

Decorate with flaked almonds.

Serve with fresh cream, hot custard or ice cream.

INGREDIENTS		
4oz/110g sugar	1 beaten egg	3 large cooking apples
4oz/110g butter	4oz/110g flour	sugar to sweeten

1. Pre-heat the oven to 180°C / 350°F / Gas Mark 4.

2. Melt the sugar and butter together in a saucepan and allow to cool.

3. Add the beaten egg. Then add all the flour and mix.

4. Stew the apples very lightly.

5. Add some sugar to sweeten the stewed apples.

6. Put the apples into a pyrex dish. Pour the cake mixture over the apples.

7. Cook in the pre-heated oven for 1 hour.

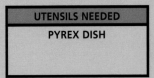

OVEN

NUMBER OF SERVINGS

PREPARATION TIME	COOKING TIME
30 minutes	**20** minutes

UTENSILS NEEDED

FLAN TIN

HANDY HINTS

Fresh fruit in season can also be used.

Fruit Flan

INGREDIENTS		
3oz/85g flour	FILLING:	small carton of cream
3oz/85g caster sugar	1 small tin of fruit	
3 eggs	1 quick-set jel or jelly	

1. Pre-heat the oven to 200°C / 400°F / Gas Mark 6.

2. Place sugar in a bowl and whisk together with eggs over a pan of hot water for 10 minutes. Remove and continue whisking for 5 minutes on table.

3. Gently fold in sieved flour, in about 4 lots.

4. Pour sponge-cake mixture into a greased and floured flan tin.

5. Bake in a pre-heated oven for approx. 20 minutes.

6. Dissolve jelly and leave in a cool place. Do not allow to set.

7. Drain the tin of fruit.

8. When flan case is cooled, arrange fruit on top and cover with jelly.

9. Allow jelly to set and decorate with piped cream.

FRIDGE **BOIL/STEW**

Fruit Salad

INGREDIENTS		
SYRUP	**FRUIT**	2 bananas
³/₄ pt/425ml water	2 apples	2 kiwi fruit
6ozs/180g sugar	2 pears	green and black grapes
juice of 1 lemon	2 oranges	

1. Dissolve the sugar in the water, bring to the boil and add the lemon juice. Pour into a bowl and allow to cool.

2. Wash the apples. Cut in thin slices and put into the syrup. Peel the pears and kiwi fruit and place them in the syrup also.

3. Peel the oranges and cut into segments and add to the bowl.

4. Slice the grapes in half and remove pips before adding them to the syrup.

5. Mix all the fruit carefully.

6. Cover the bowl with cling film and place in the fridge for 1-2 hours.

7. Peel the bananas, slice them, sprinkle with lemon juice and add to the salad shortly before serving.

COST	HEALTHY

NUMBER OF SERVINGS

PREPARATION TIME	COOKING TIME
20 minutes	

UTENSILS NEEDED

SERVING DISH

HANDY HINTS

Use a little orange juice with a few teaspoons of lemon juice added to it instead of syrup.

83

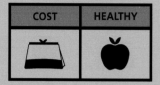

PREPARATION TIME	COOKING TIME
30 minutes	**1¾** hours

UTENSILS NEEDED
LOAF TIN OR CIRCULAR TIN

HANDY HINTS
Useful for school lunches.

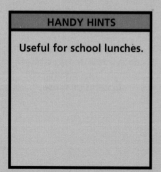

Irish Tea Brack

INGREDIENTS		
1 cup of strong tea 6oz/180g brown sugar 9ozs/250g plain flour	1lb/450g mixed dried fruit 1 egg (lightly beaten)	½ level teaspoon breadsoda

1. Pre-heat the oven to 180°C / 350°F / Gas Mark 4.

2. Put tea, sugar and dried fruit in a bowl, cover and leave to soak overnight.

3. Grease a 2lb loaf tin.

4. Add the lightly beaten egg to the fruit mixture.

5. Sieve the flour and breadsoda together and fold into mixture.

6. Turn into the prepared tin. Place in the pre-heated oven and bake for 1½ to 1¾ hours.

7. Cool on a wire tray and serve sliced with butter.

Jam Swiss Roll

INGREDIENTS		
4oz/110g margarine (at room temp.) 6oz/180g caster sugar 4 large eggs	6oz/180g self-raising flour, sieved	**FILLING & DECORATION:** warmed jam caster and icing sugar

NUMBER OF SERVINGS

PREPARATION TIME	COOKING TIME
30 minutes	**12** minutes

① Pre-heat the oven to 200°C / 400°F / Gas Mark 6.

② Place all the ingredients for the cake in a mixing bowl and beat with a wooden spoon until well mixed. (2 - 3 minutes).

③ Prepare the tin, by lining it with greaseproof paper.

④ Put the mixture in the greased and lined swiss roll tin.

⑤ Bake in the middle of the pre-heated oven for 10 - 12 minutes.

WHEN BAKED

⑥ Place a sheet of greaseproof paper on top of a damp tea-towel.

⑦ Sprinkle lightly with caster sugar.

⑧ Turn the Swiss roll out onto the sugared paper.

⑨ Remove the paper from the bottom of the cake and trim the edges of the cake.

⑩ Spread quickly with warmed jam and roll up using the greaseproof paper as a guide.

⑪ When cold unwrap and sprinkle with icing sugar.

⑫ If liked, mark the top with diagonal lines, using a hot skewer.

UTENSILS NEEDED

SWISS ROLL TIN
11" X 7"

HANDY HINTS

For a chocolate swiss roll simply replace 1 oz of flour with 1oz of drinking chocolate or cocoa.

OVEN | **BOIL/STEW**

COST | **HEALTHY**

NUMBER OF SERVINGS

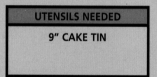

PREPARATION TIME	COOKING TIME
20 minutes	**2** hours

UTENSILS NEEDED

9" CAKE TIN

HANDY HINTS

To make a boiled fruit cake substitute the guinness with water.

Porter Cake

INGREDIENTS		
5oz/140g margarine	3oz/85g candied peel	½ teaspoon of bread soda
5oz/140g brown sugar	14oz/400g flour	
1 cup of guinness	2 eggs beaten	1½ teaspoons cinnamon
1lb/450g sultanas		

1. Pre-heat the oven to 160°C / 325°F / Gas Mark 3.

2. Put the margarine, sugar and guinness into a saucepan and boil gently. Stir the mixture until the margarine is melted and sugar dissolved. Add the fruit and candied peel and let everything simmer for 5 minutes. Allow to cool.

3. Meanwhile sieve flour, bread soda and cinnamon into a bowl. Make a well in the centre and add the beaten eggs.

4. Add the cooled mixture from the saucepan and mix together quickly and well.

5. Turn into a lined and greased 9" cake tin. Bake in the pre-heated oven for 1½ - 2 hours.

Queen Cakes

INGREDIENTS		
8oz/225g soft margarine	16oz/450g self-raising flour	a little milk
4 eggs	8oz/225g caster sugar	

1. Pre-heat the oven to 200°C / 400°F / Gas Mark 6.

2. Sieve flour into bowl.

3. Cream the margarine and sugar together.

4. Beat the eggs.

5. Add the flour and eggs gradually to the creamed margarine and sugar, beating well to avoid curdling.

6. If the mixture is dry add a little milk.

7. Divide the mixture into bun cases.

8. Bake in the pre-heated oven for 20 minutes.

OVEN

COST

NUMBER OF SERVINGS

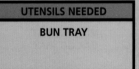

PREPARATION TIME	COOKING TIME
20 minutes	**20** minutes

UTENSILS NEEDED

BUN TRAY

HANDY HINTS

Makes 4 dozen small buns.

Add some sultanas or cherries to the mixture for variety.

These buns freeze well.

If soft margarine is used all the ingredients can be beaten together.

OVEN

COST	HEALTHY

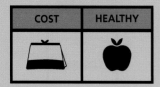

NUMBER OF SERVINGS

PREPARATION TIME	COOKING TIME
20 minutes	**20** minutes

UTENSILS NEEDED

MIXING BOWL
BAKING TRAY

HANDY HINTS

Any type of jam can be used.

Raspberry Buns

INGREDIENTS		
12ozs/340g self-raising flour 4ozs/110g sugar 2ozs/50g margarine	2 eggs pinch of salt 4 dessertspoons milk raspberry jam	2 dessertspoons water 1 teaspoon caster sugar for dusting

1. Pre-heat the oven to 230°C / 450°F / Gas Mark 8.

2. Sift the flour, salt and baking powder into a bowl. Rub in the margarine. Add the sugar and mix well.

3. Beat the eggs with the milk until light and lemon-coloured. Stir this into the flour mixture, mixing with a knife to get a smooth dough. (If dough seems slightly dry add cold water carefully a little at a time).

4. Roll dough on a lightly floured board into a thick roll, and divide in 12 equal portions.

5. Flour hands lightly and roll each portion into a ball. Place 2 inches apart on a greased baking sheet. Make a hole in the top of each bun and push in a little jam. Wet the edges of each hole and pinch together.

6. Brush with milk or egg and dust each bun over with caster sugar.

7. Bake in the pre-heated oven for 15 to 20 minutes.

'ponge Tray Bake - basic all-in-one

INGREDIENTS		
8oz/225g soft margarine 8oz/225g caster sugar	4 dessertspoons milk 12oz/300g self-raising flour	4 eggs

1. Pre-heat the oven to 180°C / 350°F / Gas Mark 4.

2. Grease and base line a 12 x 9 inch (30 x 23cm) baking tray with greased greaseproof paper.

3. Measure all the ingredients into a large bowl and beat well for about 2 minutes until well blended.
   Turn the mixture into the prepared tin and level the top.

4. Bake in the pre-heated oven for about 35-40 minutes or until the cake has shrunk from the sides of the tin and springs back when pressed in the centre with your fingertips.
   Leave to cool in the tin.

5. Cut into slices.

NUMBER OF SERVINGS

PREPARATION TIME
30 minutes

COOKING TIME
40 minutes

UTENSILS NEEDED
SWISS ROLL TIN
11" X 7" OR CIRCULAR TIN

HANDY HINTS
For handy apple slices add some chopped apples to the mixture before baking.

OVEN

COST	HEALTHY
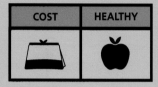	

NUMBER OF SERVINGS

PREPARATION TIME	COOKING TIME
20 minutes	**20** minutes

UTENSILS NEEDED

BAKING TRAY

HANDY HINTS

To make fruit scones add 2oz/50g mixed fruit to the mixture before adding the beaten eggs and water.

Tea Scones

INGREDIENTS		
1lb/450g self-raising flour 2oz/50g sugar	4oz/110g margarine 1 egg	water/milk

① Pre-heat the oven to 200°C / 375°F / Gas Mark 6.

② Put flour and sugar into a mixing bowl. Rub in the margarine.

③ Add the beaten eggs with sufficient water/milk to make a nice soft dough.

④ Put on a floured surface and roll to $^1/_2$ inch thickness. Cut with a knife or pastry cutter, brush over with egg wash or a little milk and put on a floured baking tray.

⑤ Bake in the pre-heated oven for 15-20 minutes.

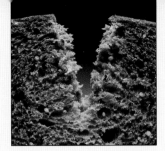

Wholemeal Bread

OVEN

INGREDIENTS		
1lb/425g wholemeal flour 1 dessertspoon wheatgerm 1 dessertspoon bran	½ pt/275ml butter milk 1 teaspoon breadsoda 1 teaspoon brown sugar	1 teaspoon salt 2 teaspoons polyunsaturated oil 1 egg (optional)

1. Pre-heat the oven to 180°C / 350°F / Gas Mark 4.

2. Mix all the ingredients well together.
   Then pour the lot into a lightly oiled loaf tin.

3. Bake in the pre-heated oven for 15 minutes.

4. Reduce heat to 150°C / 300°F / Gas Mark 2 and bake for a further 40 minutes.

COST	HEALTHY

NUMBER OF SERVINGS

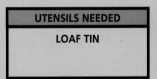

PREPARATION TIME	COOKING TIME
30 minutes	**55** minutes

UTENSILS NEEDED

LOAF TIN

HANDY HINTS

In an electric oven you can turn off the heat for the last 5 to 10 minutes and leave bread in oven to finish baking.

OVEN

COST	HEALTHY
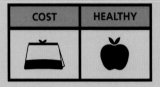	

NUMBER OF SERVINGS

PREPARATION TIME	COOKING TIME
20 minutes	**20** minutes

UTENSILS NEEDED

BAKING TRAY

Wholemeal Scones

INGREDIENTS		
6ozs/180g wholemeal flour	½ pt/275ml fresh milk	1 dessertspoon caster sugar (optional)
7oz/200g plain flour	1 teaspoon baking powder	
2oz/50g margarine	pinch of salt	

1　Pre-heat the oven to 200°C / 400°F / Gas Mark 6.

2　Place wholemeal flour, plain flour and sugar in a mixing bowl. Sieve in the salt and baking powder and mix well.

3　Rub in the margarine.

4　Add enough milk to make a soft dough. Turn onto a lightly floured board and gently knead. Roll out dough to ½ inch in thickness. Using a 2 inch cutter, shape scones and place on a baking sheet which has been dusted with flour.

5　Bake in the pre-heated oven for approx. 20 minutes.

Snacks

Packed Lunch
Choose one item from each box

1. FRUIT

- Apple
- Mandarin
- Banana
- Strawberry
- Any other fruit

2. BREAD

- Wholemeal bread
- Brown/white soda bread
- Brown/white bread
- French stick
- Pitta bread
- Scones
- Banana bread

3. FILLINGS

- Tuna and sweetcorn
- Cold chicken mashed in natural yoghurt and cucumber
- Sliced ham and tomato sauce and lettuce
- Hard boiled eggs mixed with onion in natural yoghurt and lettuce
- Curried tuna and lettuce
- Grated low-fat cheese with tomato and lettuce
- Peanut butter and banana

4. DRINK

- Milk
- Yoghurt
- Flavoured milk
- Fruit juice
- Homemade soup

Alternative suggestions for packed lunches

1. **Salad Box**
   Egg, lettuce, tomato, onion, cucumber, coleslaw

2. **Pasta Dishes**
   Pasta, tuna and sweetcorn
   Pasta, tomato and ham

3. **Chicken drumsticks and salad**

4. **Cream crackers and low-fat cheese**

GRILL　**OVEN**

NUMBER OF SERVINGS

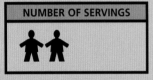

PREPARATION TIME	COOKING TIME
5 minutes	**10** minutes

UTENSILS NEEDED

HANDY HINTS

Use brown bread for healthier option.

Add some grated onion for flavour.

Bacon Surprise

INGREDIENTS		
4 slices white or brown bread	4oz/110g grated cheese	4 back rashers or 4 streaky rashers
butter		

1　Cut off crusts of bread. Roll out bread thinly.

2　Spread lightly with butter.

3　Put 1oz/25g grated cheese on each slice of bread and roll up tightly.

4　Wrap each roll with a rasher and grill until golden brown or bake in the oven.

Baked Potato with Fillings

INGREDIENTS		
2 large potatoes scrubbed but not peeled	1 dessertspoon vegetable oil	

1. Pre-heat the oven to 220°C / 425°F / Gas Mark 7.

2. Wash the potatoes, then prick them all over with a fork. Coat with a little oil until the skin is shiny.

3. Bake in a pre-heated oven for 1¹/₂ hours or until the inside is tender.

4. For the microwave method, follow the instructions given in the manual.

FILLINGS FOR BAKED POTATO

BACON AND SWEETCORN FILLING:

2 large baked potatoes	4 rashers
6 dessertspoons tinned sweetcorn	salt and pepper

1. Grill the rashers and cut into small pieces.
2. Cut the potato in half and carefully scoop the centre out of the potato.
3. Mix this potato with the sweetcorn, rashers, salt and pepper.
4. Return the mixture to potato skin.
5. Place in a hot oven and bake until warmed through and golden.

COST

HEALTHY

NUMBER OF SERVINGS

PREPARATION TIME	COOKING TIME
10 minutes	**20** minutes

UTENSILS NEEDED

OVEN TRAY

HANDY HINTS

Par-boil the potatoes in their skins for about 20 minutes, then prick them and cover them with oil and bake for 15 minutes in a conventional oven. 180°C / 350°F / Gas Mark 4.

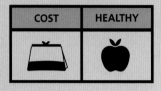

Baked Potato with Fillings
(continued)

SAVOURY MINCED BEEF AND TOMATO FILLING

2 large baked potatoes	4oz/110g minced beef
1 medium onion	1 dessertspoon tomato puree
salt and pepper	tomato slices for garnish

1. Fry the minced beef, onion and tomato puree until well cooked.
2. Cut the potato in half and carefully scoop the centre out of the potato.
3. Mix this potato with the mince, add salt and pepper.
4. Return the mixture to the potato skins.
5. Place in a hot oven and bake until warmed through and slightly browned on top.
6. Garnish with tomato slices.

TUNA AND POTATO FILLING

2 large baked potatoes	7oz/200g can tuna fish, flaked
salt and pepper	4oz/110g back bacon, grilled until crisp, crumbled

1. Cut the potato in half and carefully scoop the centre out of the potato.
2. Mix this potato, tuna and chopped bacon together.
3. Add a little salt and pepper
4. Return the mixture to the potato skins.
5. Place in a hot oven and bake until warmed through and slightly browned on top.

TURKEY AND HAM TOPPING

2 large baked potatoes	4oz/110g cooked turkey	mayonnaise
4oz/110g cooked ham	1 dessertspoon of peas	

1. Cut the potato in half and carefully scoop the centre out of the potato.
2. Slice the turkey and ham and add to the mashed potato flesh.
3. Stir in peas and a little mayonnaise.
4. Add a little salt and pepper.
5. Return the mixture to the potato skins.
6. Place in a hot oven and bake until warmed through and slightly browned on top.

French Bread Pizza

INGREDIENTS		
1 french baguette, cut in half black pepper	2 tomatoes, sliced 2 dessertspoons (30 ml) tomato sauce	2oz/50g cheese, grated

1. Pre-heat the grill.

2. Spread the tomato sauce over the cut surfaces of the baguette.

3. Top with slices of tomato and season with black pepper.

4. Sprinkle with the cheese.

5. Grill for about 2 minutes until the cheese has melted and is beginning to bubble.

GRILL

COST

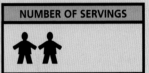

NUMBER OF SERVINGS

PREPARATION TIME	**COOKING TIME**
5 minutes	**2** minutes

UTENSILS NEEDED

HANDY HINTS

Cooked ham, peppers, mushrooms can also be used.

COST	HEALTHY

NUMBER OF SERVINGS

PREPARATION TIME	COOKING TIME
10 minutes	**20** minutes

UTENSILS NEEDED

LARGE PIE DISH

HANDY HINTS

Any type of pasta can be used.

Macaroni Cheese

INGREDIENTS		
6oz/180g quick-cooking macaroni cheese sauce (page 13) salt	TOPPING: 2oz/50g grated cheddar cheese	2oz/50g brown breadcrumbs

1. Pre-heat the oven to 180°C / 350°F / Gas Mark 4.

2. Cook macaroni in boiling salted water and drain.

3. Make the cheese sauce. (See sauces, page 13)

4. Add cooked macaroni to cheese sauce and pour into a large pie dish. Top with grated cheese and breadcrumbs.

5. Bake in the pre-heated oven for 20 mins.

6. Serve with triangles of toast.

Pancakes

INGREDIENTS		
8oz/225g flour 1 egg	³/₄ pt/425ml milk pinch salt	

1. Sieve flour and salt into a bowl.

2. Make a hole in the centre of the flour and drop in the egg with 4 dessertspoons of milk.

3. Stir the egg mixture in the centre of the bowl with a wooden spoon, allowing the flour to fall in gradually from the sides.

4. Add the rest of the milk slowly, beating well to avoid lumping.

SWEET FILLINGS:
Stewed apples
Jam
Fried bananas

SAVOURY FILLINGS:
Chopped cooked chicken
Smoked haddock
Tinned salmon
Mushrooms
Stirred in and cooked in white sauce

OTHER:
Mince cooked
in curry sauce
Bolognese sauce

FRY

COST

NUMBER OF SERVINGS

PREPARATION TIME	COOKING TIME
10 minutes	**15** minutes

UTENSILS NEEDED
BOWL
FRYING PAN

HANDY HINTS
Serve with caster sugar &
lemon juice.

GRILL

OVEN

COST	HEALTHY

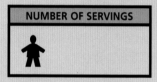

NUMBER OF SERVINGS

PREPARATION TIME	COOKING TIME
5 minutes	**3** minutes

UTENSILS NEEDED

BAKING TRAY

Pizza Baps

INGREDIENTS		
a brown or white bap tomato, thinly sliced ½ onion, sliced	2oz/50g grated cheese 2 mushrooms (optional)	

1. Lightly brown the bap under the grill until softened and warm, then cut in half.

2. Cook 2 slices of onion in a little oil and add sliced mushrooms if you wish.

3. Slice a tomato thinly and arrange on the two sides of the bap and pop the onions and mushrooms on top.

4. Sprinkle the grated cheese on top.

5. Bake in a pre-heated oven 180°C / 350°F / Gas Mark 4, or grill until golden brown for a few minutes.

Pizza Quick

GRILL | OVEN

INGREDIENTS		
SCONE BASE:	a little milk	4 mushrooms
7oz/200g self-raising flour	1 dessertspoon oil	6 tomatoes / 1 tin of tomatoes
3oz/85g margarine	1 onion	2oz/50g grated cheese
pinch of salt		

COST | **HEALTHY**

NUMBER OF SERVINGS

PREPARATION TIME	COOKING TIME
15 minutes	**30** minutes

UTENSILS NEEDED

BAKING TRAY

HANDY HINTS

Any variety of vegetables or cooked meat can be used to top the pizza.

Serve with salad.

1. Pre-heat the oven to 200°C / 400°F / Gas Mark 6.

2. Heat the oil in a frying pan, cook the chopped onion and mushrooms for 3-5 minutes. Add the chopped tomatoes. (If using tinned tomatoes add the juice as well). Simmer gently for 5 minutes.

3. Sieve the flour and salt into a bowl. Rub in the margarine.

4. Add the milk and mix to a stiff ball. Roll into a large round $1/2''$ in thickness.

5. Place on a greased tin.

6. Spread the tomato mixture on the base and sprinkle cheese on top.

7. Bake in the pre-heated oven for 30 minutes.

PREPARATION TIME	COOKING TIME
20 minutes	**10** minutes

UTENSILS NEEDED

FRYING PAN

HANDY HINTS

Serve with hot beans.

A handy way to use leftover potatoes.

Mixed herbs and chopped onion can be added for variety.

Potato Cakes

INGREDIENTS		
2oz/55g flour pinch salt ¼ teaspoon baking powder	3 potatoes, cooked and mashed ½oz/15g melted butter or margarine	3 dessertspoons vegetable oil

1. Sieve together flour, salt and baking powder.

2. Add the mashed potatoes and melted butter.

3. Bind together, using milk if necessary.

4. Turn onto a floured board or clean table top. Knead until the mixture is smooth.

5. Divide in two equal parts.

6. Flatten each piece with your hand to form a circle and cut into eight triangles.

7. Cook on a well-oiled, hot pan until brown on both sides.

Quiches - Various

INGREDIENTS-PASTRY		
6oz/180g plain flour 3oz/85g margarine	pinch of salt a little water	or 1 packet of frozen shortcrust pastry

PASTRY

1. Sieve the flour and salt into a bowl.

2. Rub in the chopped margarine until the mixture resembles fine breadcrumbs.

3. Add the water and mix to a stiff dough.

4. Roll out the pastry and line a flan dish.

SUGGESTIONS FOR FILLINGS:

1. Salmon and tomato

2. Bacon and mushroom

3. Quiche Lorraine

OVEN

COST

NUMBER OF SERVINGS

PREPARATION TIME	COOKING TIME
20 minutes	**45** minutes

UTENSILS NEEDED

FLAN DISH
OVEN DISH

HANDY HINTS

For a rich quiche substitute cream for some of the milk.

Use a cooked vegetable for a quick filling.

OVEN

COST

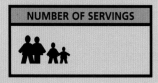

NUMBER OF SERVINGS

PREPARATION TIME	COOKING TIME
20 minutes	**45** minutes

UTENSILS NEEDED

FLAN DISH
OVEN DISH

HANDY HINTS

For a rich quiche substitute some of the milk for cream.

Quiche Fillings

BACON AND MUSHROOM:

2 back rashers	4 mushrooms	salt and pepper
2 eggs	1/3 pt/200ml milk	2oz/50g grated cheese

Mix the eggs, milk, pepper and salt together. Grill the bacon and mushrooms, and allow to cool. Then chop them roughly and arrange on ba of the flan. Pour the egg mixture over the bacon and mushrooms. Sprinkle little grated cheese on top. Bake in the oven.

SALMON AND TOMATO:

1 tin of salmon	2 tomatoes	2 eggs
salt and pepper	grated cheese	1/3 pt/200ml milk

Drain the salmon and remove the bones. Slice the tomatoes. Arrange salmo and tomato on base of the flan case. Mix together the eggs, milk, pepper an salt and pour over the salmon and tomatoes. Sprinkle a little grated cheese the top. Bake in the oven.

QUICHE LORRAINE:

4 back rashers	2oz/50g grated cheese	1/3 pt/200ml milk
2 eggs	salt and pepper	

Grill the bacon and chop roughly. Place in the flan case. Mix together the milk, eggs, pepper, salt and pour over the bacon. Sprinkle the grated cheese top and bake in the oven.

BAKE IN A PRE-HEATED OVEN 200°C / 400°F/ GAS MARK 6 FOR 40-45 MINUTES.

Tea-Time Scramble

INGREDIENTS		
3 eggs	1 tomato, chopped	salt and pepper
2 dessertspoons of milk	2oz/50g cooked ham, chopped	2 slices hot buttered toast
1/4oz/5g butter or margarine	2oz/50g cheddar cheese, grated	parsley to garnish

1. Beat eggs and milk together. Pour into a saucepan.

2. Add butter, chopped tomato and ham, grated cheese and seasoning.

3. Cook over a low heat until creamy, stirring all the time.

4. Spoon equal portions on to the toast.

5. Sprinkle with chopped parsley and serve hot.

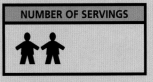

COST	HEALTHY

NUMBER OF SERVINGS

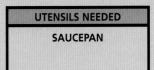

PREPARATION TIME	COOKING TIME
10 minutes	**10** minutes

UTENSILS NEEDED

SAUCEPAN

107

GRILL

COST	HEALTHY
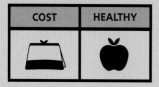	

NUMBER OF SERVINGS

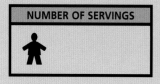

PREPARATION TIME	COOKING TIME
5 minutes	**2** minutes

UTENSILS NEEDED

HANDY HINTS

Use worcestershire sauce instead of mustard.

Toasted Cheese

INGREDIENTS		
2 slices bread 2oz/50g cheese	2 teaspoons soft margarine or butter	1 teaspoon french mustard

① Pre-heat the grill. Toast the bread on one side.

② Toast the other side until it crisps but has not turned brown.

③ Mash the cheese, margarine and mustard together and spread over the toast.

④ Grill for about 2 minutes until bubbling and starting to brown.

TOASTED CHEESE AND TOMATO:
As above, but add 2 teaspoons tomato puree to the cheese mixture before toasting.

TOASTED CHEESE AND PICKLE:
As in main recipe, but add 2 teaspoons of your favourite pickle to the cheese mixture before toasting.

Weaning

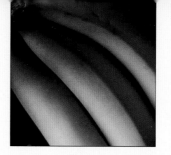

Suggested Guide to Weaning

	6 months	7-9 months	9-12 months
Cereal	Start with 1 teaspoon of baby rice. It should be of a thick liquid consistency and easy for the baby to swallow.	Mixed cereal based on wheat, oats, rye and barley.	Regular cereals, i.e., wheat biscuit. Avoid sugar-coated cereals.
Bread		Fingers of toast/bread, rusks.	Fingers of toast/bread, rusk
Vegetables	Carrot, potato, cauliflower: simmer them and then liquidise or sieve them. (Avoid tinned vegetable).	Stronger flavoured vegetable: cabbage, sprouts, turnips. Simmer them, then mash or mince them.	Mash, mince or chop vegetables at this stage. Baked beans can be introduced.
Fruit	Mash bananas, stew fresh fruit and liquidise or sieve them, i.e., apples, pears. Tinned fruit in juice can also be used.	Mash raw fruit.	Mince or chop fruit finely this age.
Eggs		Scrambled or hard boiled eggs. Add to vegetables or cereal.	Scrambled or hard boiled eggs. Add to vegetables or cereal.
Yoghurt		Plain yoghurts with a little pureed fruit.	Plain yoghurts with a little pureed fruit.
Cheese		Soft cheese or grated mild cheese.	Soft cheese or grated mild cheese.
Meat Poultry		Finely chopped meat without salt or spice. Moisten with home-made stock.	Mince or chop.
Fish		White fish grilled, baked or steamed. Always remove the bones.	Fish fingers or other frozen fish products. Tinned salmon or tuna could be tried. Remove bones.

Hints & Recipes for Baby Foods

To Freeze

Spoon the prepared food into plastic ice cube trays. Allow to cool. Freeze food cubes, pop out and put into freezer bags. Label and date. As the baby gets older use larger containers (e.g. yoghurt or margarine cartons).

AVOID the following when preparing food for your baby

Packet soups
Packet sauce mixes
Butter or margarine in large amounts

Stock cubes, Gravy
All savoury mixes with high salt content.

To moisten baby foods use

UNDER 6 MONTHS:
Breast milk or
formula milk if not breast feeding
Water
Pure fruit juice
Home-made stock

7 MONTHS ONWARDS:
Milk
Thin white sauce
Thin custard
Plain natural yoghurt

BOIL/STEW

COST	HEALTHY
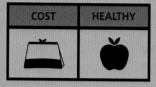	

NUMBER OF SERVINGS

PREPARATION TIME	COOKING TIME
10 minutes	**30** minutes

UTENSILS NEEDED

SAUCEPAN
SIEVE

HANDY HINTS

* Vegetable water can also be used for moistening baby food.

Use liquidisers to puree vegetables and chicken.

Use remainder of stock for soup.

Chicken and Rice
(from 7 months)

INGREDIENTS		
75g/3oz chicken fillets ½ cup of rice	50g/2oz mixed vegetables e.g., carrots, parsnips, etc.	¼ pt/150ml water

1. Cut chicken fillets into small pieces.

2. Wash, peel and chop mixed vegetables.

3. Simmer the chicken and vegetables in the water for 20-30 minutes until tender. Save the stock.

4. Cook rice in boiling water for 10-12 minutes.

5. Strain the rice in the sieve and pour boiling water through to remove starch.

6. Mix the chicken, rice and vegetables together. Add a little stock to moisten*. Mash or puree.

Fish Surprise
(from 7 months)

INGREDIENTS		
1oz/25g margarine/butter ¼ pt/150ml milk	1 dessertspoon plain flour 4oz/110g cooked white fish*	2 dessertspoons frozen peas (cooked)

1. Melt the margarine or butter in a saucepan, stir in the flour and cook for two minutes.

2. Gradually add the milk, stirring continuously.

3. Bring to the boil slowly. Remove from the heat.

4. Flake the fish and mash with the peas. Add in the white sauce gradually according to desired texture and flavour.

COST	HEALTHY

NUMBER OF SERVINGS

PREPARATION TIME	COOKING TIME
10 minutes	**10** minutes

UTENSILS NEEDED

SAUCEPAN

HANDY HINTS

*Tinned salmon or tuna may be used instead of the white fish. Always remove the bones and drain tinned fish.

Cook the fish on a plate over the saucepan in which the peas are cooking.

COST	HEALTHY

NUMBER OF SERVINGS

PREPARATION TIME	COOKING TIME
10 minutes	**30** minutes

UTENSILS NEEDED

CASSEROLE DISH
A BLENDER IF AVAILABLE

HANDY HINTS

Try different shapes and colours to add variety to dish.

Pasta and Cheese
(from 7 months)

INGREDIENTS		
1 egg 3oz/75g cottage cheese $^1/_4$ pt/150ml of milk	1 dessertspoon grated cheddar cheese	1 cup cooked pasta (e.g., macaroni)

1. Pre-heat the oven to 180°C / 350°F / Gas Mark 4.

2. Beat the egg. Add milk and cheeses, mixing well. (A blender is ideal).

3. Add to the cooked pasta.

4. Pour into a lightly greased casserole dish.

5. Bake in the oven for about 30 minutes.

Savoury Potatoes
(from 7 months)

INGREDIENTS		
potatoes	cauliflower	cottage cheese
vegetables	peas	grated cheese
carrot	broccoli	

1 Boil potatoes in their skins and peel afterwards.

2 Mash potato flesh and add a little milk,
adding one or more of the following:
- mashed cooked vegetable like carrot, cauliflower, peas, broccoli;
- cottage cheese;
- grated cheese.

COST	HEALTHY

NUMBER OF SERVINGS

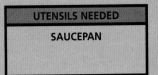

PREPARATION TIME	COOKING TIME
10 minutes	**10** minutes

UTENSILS NEEDED

SAUCEPAN

HANDY HINTS

Ideal for children to make.

Use a microwave for cooking potatoes and vegetables.

Young People

Benefits of Healthy Eating!

- Keep your body in great shape
- Clear, healthy skin
- Shiny, healthy hair
- Healthy happy heart
- Great smile and strong bones
- Be the best you can be at sports
- Have a great memory and make learning easier

Just Do It!

- Beat the morning blues!
  Breakfast is the most important meal of the day!

- 1. Breakfast   2. Lunch   3. Dinner - GO!!!

- When hunger attacks - Strike back with a Healthy Snack!

- Thirsty Teenagers -
  Try Tasty Healthy Drinks!

- V - Variety   B - Balance   P - Portions!

Remember: *Use the following tables as a guide for choosing meals and snacks.*

Mix & Match for Meal Planning

Mix and match foods from the colour code below when planning your meals.

Green: = Go Foods - Eat to your hearts content!!
Orange: = Caution Foods - Enjoy foods from here but don't go wild!
Red: = Easy-Does-It - Enjoy these foods as a treat!

	Green	Orange	Red
Cereal	• High fibre cereals • Porridge	• Plain cereals	• Chocolate/sugar coated cereals
Bread	• Brown bread	• All white bread	• Bread with large amounts of spreads/jams/butter
Potatoes	• Boiled/steamed or baked potatoes	• Potatoes: roast/mashed • Homemade spicy wedges	• Chips
Rice	• Brown boiled rice	• White boiled rice	• Fried rice
Pasta	• Brown boiled pasta	• White boiled pasta • Plain pizza/with vegetables on	• Pasta with creamy sauce and extra cheese • Pepperoni pizza/extra cheese
Vegetables	• Fresh/frozen vegetables • Salad • Homemade vegetable soup	• Salad with small amounts of regular dressing or low fat dressing • Coleslaw-small amounts	• Salad with lots of dressing/oils • Potato salad • Packet vegetable soup
Fruit	• Fresh fruit e.g. apples, pears • Tinned fruit in natural/ own juice • Freshly squeezed juices	• Raisins/dried fruits • No added sugar/ unsweetened fruit juices	• Tinned fruit in syrup • Squash/juice drinks

Mix & Match for Meal Planning cont'd

	Green	Orange	Red
Milk	• Low fat milk • Skimmed milk • Semi-skimmed milk	• Full Fat milk	• Flavoured milk e.g. chocolate, strawberry • Ice cream

Yoghurt	• Natural yoghurts
	• Diet yoghurts
	• Yoghurt drinks
		• Yoghurt - Frozen
		            - Full fat
		            - Fruit
			• Chocolate/toffee
			  flavoured yoghurts

Cheese	• Low fat cheddar cheese
	• Cottage cheese
	• Edam/ mozzarella
		• Cheese - Full fat
		           - Mini round
		           - Plain sticks
			• Cheese spreads
			• Processed cheese

Meat/Poultry Alternatives	• Beans* • Lentils	• Lean red meat* • Chicken/turkey*	• Meat/chicken in batter or breadcrumbs • Burgers/sausage rolls • Sausages/rashers/pudding

Fish	• Fresh fish	• Tinned - In brine
		  Fish - Tomato sauce
		           - Olive oil
			• Fish in batter/
			  breadcrumbs

Eggs		Boiled/scrambled* poached	Fried

* Good healthy sources of iron. Iron is important for teenagers.

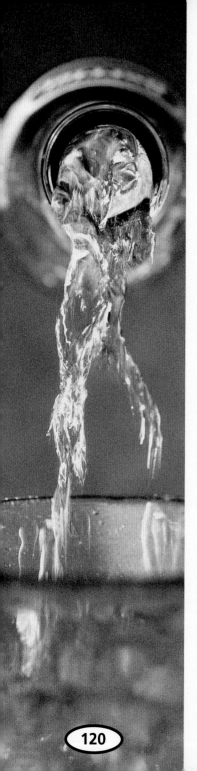

Snack Attack!!!!

Green	Orange	Red
• Fruit/Brown scones • Crackers • Brown bread • High fibre breakfast cereals • Plain popcorn	• Plain biscuits • Plain scones • Pretzels • Bagels • Rolls • Peanut butter/banana on brown bread	• Sweet/chocolate biscuits • Cookies/buns/muffins • Cakes and tarts • Ice-cream • Chocolate • Crisps • Peanuts • Chocolate spread • Salted/butter/toffee coated popcorn
• High fibre cereal bar (nuts and grains)	• Cereal bar	• Cereal bars coated with sweet layer or chocolate

• Yoghurt
  1. Natural yoghurts
  2. Diet yoghurt
  3. Yoghurt drinks
	• Frozen yoghurt
	• Full fat yoghurts
	• Low fat custard
	• Sugar free jelly
		• Chocolate/toffee flavoured yoghurts

• Fresh fruit • Vegetable sticks e.g. carrots	• Raisins/dried fruit	
• Baked potato	• Pizza • Brown bread with luncheon meat, tuna & sweet corn • Homemade oven chips • Homemade spicy wedges	• Chips • Burgers • Sausages/rashers/pudding • Sausage rolls

Quench It! - Drinks

Green	Orange	Red
• Water • Milk • Freshly squeezed juices • Homemade fruit smoothies	• Unsweetened fruit juice • No added sugar drinks/squashes • Diet/light minerals • Fruit based milky drinks • Flavoured waters • Sports energy drinks (for serious sports)	• Fizzy drinks • Sugar drinks (squash & juices) • High-energy caffeine drinks.

Fruit Smoothies

INGREDIENTS		
1-2 pieces of large fruit (e.g. apple and pear) ½ carton of low fat diet yoghurt	⅓ pt low fat milk ½ cup of freshly squeezed fruit juice	1 teaspoon of honey 4 ice cubes 2 marshmallows (optional)

1. Make sure all the ingredients are chilled before use.

2. Wash and peel fruit.

3. Blend fruit, yoghurt, milk and juice together until creamy.

4. Add honey and ice cubes and blend again.

5. Serve in a tall glass and place a marshmallow on top.

COST	HEALTHY

NUMBER OF SERVINGS

PREPARATION TIME	COOKING TIME
10 minutes	**0** minutes

UTENSILS NEEDED

LIQUIDISER/BLENDER
JUICE SQUEEZER

HANDY HINTS

Use a variety of fruit: apples, oranges, kiwi, seedless grapes, strawberry and bananas.

Use freshly squeezed orange or lemon juice.

Use low fat/diet yoghurt natural/ strawberry, orange, vanilla.

Tossed Green Salad

INGREDIENTS	
DRESSING: 3 tablespoons olive oil 1 teaspoon whole grain mustard 1 teaspoon honey 1 tablespoon of lemon juice salt and pepper	**SALAD:** 7oz/200gms mixed lettuce leaves 1/2 cucumber 3-4 tomatoes 1 medium carrot

1 DRESSING METHOD:
- Place all ingredients in jar with a secure lid.
- Make sure lid is on tightly.
- Shake well to mix ingredients together.

2 SALAD METHOD:
- Wash, drain and gently pat the lettuce leaves.
- Tear leaves into small pieces.
- Wash, dry and slice cucumber.
- Wash tomatoes and cut each into eight pieces.
- Wash, peel and grate carrot.
- Mix lettuce, cucumber and tomatoes in large bowl.

3 WHEN READY TO SERVE:
- Drizzle dressing over the salad and toss to coat.
- Sprinkle grated carrot on top.

Pesto and Chicken with Pasta

FRY

INGREDIENTS		
4 chicken fillets chopped	3 teaspoons green pesto	1 teaspoon vegetable oil
12oz/340gms pasta	salt and pepper	1 small onion chopped
1 pepper		

1. Cook the pasta as instructed on the pack.

2. Heat the olive oil in a frying pan. Add the chopped onion. Fry for 2 mins. Add the chopped chicken and fry for 8-10 mins, turning occasionally. Season with salt and pepper.

3. Chop the pepper.

4. Add the chopped pepper, pasta and pesto sauce to the chicken. Stir well. Cook for a further 5 mins.

5. Serve hot.

COST

NUMBER OF SERVINGS

PREPARATION TIME	COOKING TIME
5 minutes	**20** minutes

UTENSILS NEEDED

FRYING PAN
SAUCEPAN

HANDY HINTS

Any vegetable can be added to this dish.

Delicious sprinkled with roasted pine nuts.

COST	HEALTHY

NUMBER OF SERVINGS

PREPARATION TIME	COOKING TIME
15 minutes	**35** minutes

UTENSILS NEEDED

PLASTIC CONTAINER
BAKING TRAY
1 LARGE BOWL AND
METAL SPOON

HANDY HINTS

Serve with green salad.

Cover with natural yoghurt, low fat grated cheese or salsa.

Try other spices to alter flavours –
Cajun, Indian or Mexican, garlic.

124

Spicy Potato Wedges

INGREDIENTS		
4 medium size potatoes	1 teaspoon cayenne pepper	
2 tablespoons of vegetable oil	salt & black pepper	

1. Pre-heat the oven to 200°C/400°F/Gas Mark 6.

2. Wash and cut potatoes into 8 wedges (leave skin on).

3. Place in a container and pour vegetable oil over them. Close container and shake.

4. Sprinkle wedges with cayenne pepper, salt and pepper and close container and shake again.

5. Place wedges on baking tray.

6. Cook for 35 minutes until golden brown.

Cheese Melties

INGREDIENTS		
2 soft flour tortillas	1 teaspoon wholegrain mustard	
2oz/50g grated cheese		
1 slice of ham	1 teaspoon of vegetable oil	

1. Heat the vegetable oil in a frying pan

2. Place 1 tortilla on a dinner plate. Spread 1 teaspoon of wholegrain mustard evenly on one side.

3. Sprinkle the grated cheese on top.

4. Chop the ham into small pieces and place on top of the cheese.

5. Place the second tortilla on top, making a sandwich.

6. Put the sandwich into the hot frying pan. Using a spatula turn the sandwich immediately.

7. Cook on the reverse side for 1 minute and turn again.

8. Cut into 6 pieces. Serve with a crisp green salad.

NUMBER OF SERVINGS

PREPARATION TIME	COOKING TIME
5 minutes	**2** minutes

UTENSILS NEEDED

SPATULA
FRYING PAN
CHEESE GRATER

HANDY HINTS

If you are having a second meltie heat 1 teaspoon of oil between each sandwich.

The melties burn very easily. Take care when cooking them.

Very, very filling.

FRY

OVEN

COST

NUMBER OF SERVINGS

PREPARATION TIME	COOKING TIME
5 minutes	**15** minutes

UTENSILS NEEDED

FRYING PAN

HANDY HINTS

For a healthy option add grated carrot and/or mushrooms.

Serve with low fat natural yoghurt or sour cream.

8 chicken nuggets baked in oven instead of chicken fillets.

Chicken Tortillas

INGREDIENTS		
2 chicken fillets 1 green pepper 1 red pepper	4oz/100g grated cheese 4 tortilla wraps chicken fajita	seasoning/sauce/salsa 1 teaspoon vegetable oil

1. Cut the chicken into small strips.

2. Slice the peppers and onions into thin strips.

3. Fry the chicken in the olive oil over a medium heat for 8-10 minutes.

4. Add the fajita spice mix and vegetables.

5. Stir fry for a further 3 minutes until the seasoning mix coats them thoroughly to make a juicy filling.

6. Heat the tortillas in either:
   Oven   Pre-heat the oven to 180°C / Gas Mark 4.
   or   Wrap in tin foil and heat for 15 minutes.
   Microwave Place on a plate, cover with cling film and heat for 1 minute on full power.

7. Place the chicken mix on top of the wrap, sprinkle cheese on top and roll the tortilla around the filling to make a fajita.

8. Serve with green salad.

Baked Apples

OVEN

INGREDIENTS		
3 cooking apples 50ml water brown sugar	3 teaspoons of butter low fat natural yoghurt	

1. Pre-heat the oven to 200°C / 400°F / Gas Mark 6.

2. Wash apples and remove the core.

3. Place in a baking dish.

4. Pour the water around the apples.

5. Fill each apple with sugar and top with 1 teaspoon of butter.

6. Bake in the oven till the apples are soft - about 30 minutes.

7. Remove from baking dish and drizzle with low-fat natural yoghurt.

COST	HEALTHY

NUMBER OF SERVINGS

PREPARATION TIME 10 minutes

COOKING TIME 30 minutes

UTENSILS NEEDED

BAKING DISH

HANDY HINTS

Use mincemeat (jar) instead of sugar.

Stuff the apples with currants, sultanas, raisins or any dried fruit.

Mix grated orange rind or cloves with the brown sugar.

Can be cooked in the Microwave.

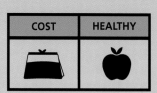

COST	HEALTHY

NUMBER OF SERVINGS

PREPARATION TIME	COOKING TIME
5 minutes	

UTENSILS NEEDED

AIR TIGHT CONTAINER - LUNCH BOX

HANDY HINTS

You can make enough for a week or according to your budget.

Buy the broken nuts in the Health shops as they are cheaper.

"A Graze Box"

INGREDIENTS		
100gms of dried fruit - raisins, sultanas, apricots etc	100gms of nuts - sunflower seeds, almonds, shelled nuts, cashews, hazelnuts	

1. Place ingredients into an airtight container.

2. Put on lid and shake well mixing all the flavours of the nuts and dried fruit together.

3. Store in a cool dry place.

4. Eat within 14 days of preparation.

Ideal to munch on looking at TV, studying or just grazing!

CAUTION: This is not suitable for children under 5 years of age.

Other meal & snack suggestions

Meals

Chilli Con Carne
Page 20

Spanish Omelette
Page 61

Stir-Fry Vegetables
Page 62

Veggie Burger
Page 63

Snacks

Baked Potato
Page 97

Pizza Baps
Page 108

Tea-Time scramble
Page 107

Toasted Cheese
Page 108

Hygiene in the Domestic Kitchen

1. Purchase food from a reliable source. Check the "sell by", "use by" and "best before" dates.

2. Put refrigerated foods and frozen foods into your fridge or freezer as soon as possible after buying.

3. Do not overload your fridge or freezer.

4. Do not store raw and cooked foods on the same shelf. Place cooked and ready-to-eat foods on a shelf higher than uncooked foods to prevent juices from raw meat coming into contact with other food.

5. Do not handle food unnecessarily.

6. Wash raw fruit and vegetables thoroughly before eating.

7. Cook food thoroughly. Cooked food should be kept clean and covered.

8. When re-heating food ensure that it is piping hot all the way through before eating. Food should never be re-heated more than once.

9. Surfaces and utensils should be cleaned with hot water and detergent before and after use.

Hygiene in the Domestic Kitchen

0) All kitchen cloths should be boiled frequently and replaced regularly.
Use carefully, remembering where they were last used.
Tea towels should not be used as hand towels or wipe cloths.

1) Keep family pets outside the kitchen.
Their food should be kept separate from family food and different utensils
and crockery should be used to feed them.

2) All rubbish should be stored in a rubbish bag or bin and sealed tightly
when full. Waste should always be kept covered and rubbish bags should
be removed daily to an outdoor bin.

3) Wash your hands thoroughly:
- Before preparing food,
- After handling raw meat and vegetables,
- After coughing, sneezing or using a handkerchief,
- After handling a baby's nappy,
- After handling pets.

4) Cover any cuts and scars with water-proof dressing.

General Freezing and Thawing

- All frozen foods should be properly sealed.

- The freezer should be maintained at a temperature of -18°C or less, check that the freezer is in good working order.

- Frozen food must not be stored for longer than recommended by the manufacturer.

- Never use hot water or other artificial means to thaw frozen food.

- Always make sure that frozen foods are completely thawed especially chicken before cooking (unless the instructions specifically state "cook from frozen", e.g., frozen vegetables).

- Frozen foods should be defrosted in a fridge.

- The freezer should be defrosted on a regular basis to prevent the build-up of ice.

- Label food with food type, date and weight.

- Never refreeze food unless it has first been cooked.

- Avoid putting hot food in a freezer.

Shopping Guide

1. Set aside the amount of money you can spend on food each week.

2. Write out a shopping list. Plan menus for a few days ahead; it will save money as you are less likely to buy food on impulse.

3. The more expensive brands are usually displayed at eye level; check the top and bottom shelves for special offers and cheaper brands.

4. Supermarkets' own brands are cheaper. They are often made by the same company as the 'advertised' brands.

5. Pound for pound, potatoes are cheaper than ready-made chips but they take time to prepare.

6. Fruit and vegetables tend to be cheaper in grocery shops than in the supermarkets.

Shopping Guide

(7) Cheapest vegetables are usually cabbage, carrots, cauliflower, broccoli, mixed vegetables (frozen) and frozen peas.

(8) When fresh vegetables are not in season frozen or tinned ones will be cheaper and are just as good.

(9) Eggs are easy to cook and full of nourishment.
DO NOT EAT RAW EGGS.

(10) Meat is cheaper in a butcher's shop than the supermarket and you can choose the exact amount you want.

(11) Mince is low in cost and it has no waste from bone and gristle.
Mince may be high in fat.
It is better to buy a smaller quantity of leaner mince.

(12) Fish is quick to prepare and very nutritious. Different varieties of fish, such as mackerel, coley, herrings, fish fingers and tinned fish, are good value for money.